A Restless Soul

OTHER BOOKS BY HENRI J.M. NOUWEN

published by Ave Maria Press

BEHOLD THE BEAUTY OF THE LORD

CAN YOU DRINK THE CUP?

THE DANCE OF LIFE
edited by Michael Ford

ETERNAL SEASONS
edited by Michael Ford

HEART SPEAKS TO HEART

IN MEMORIAM

OUT OF SOLITUDE

WITH OPEN HANDS

Learn more about Henri Nouwen, his writing, and the work of the Henri Nouwen Society at www.HenriNouwen.org.

A Restless Soul

MEDITATIONS FROM THE ROAD

HENRI J.M. NOUWEN
Edited by
Michael Ford

ave maria press AmP notre dame, indiana

First published by Darton, Longman and Todd, London, UK

Founded in 1865, Ave Maria Press is a ministry of the Indiana Province of Holy Cross.

www.avemariapress.com

ISBN-10 1-59471-163-1 ISBN-13 978-1-59471-163-3

Cover and text design by David R. Scholtes

Printed and bound in the United States of America.

For

Dr. David Torevell

It is close to midnight. My flight is leaving at 1:00 a.m. At 6:30 a.m. I will be in Miami, at 10:15 a.m. in Washington D.C., and at 2:05 p.m. in Rochester, New York. If all goes well, I will be at the abbey around 3:30 p.m., just in time to celebrate the Eucharist with the monks. It is hard for me to comprehend this huge step from a restless airport in Peru to the restful monastery in upstate New York. My mind cannot yet do what the plane will do.

¡GRACIAS!

Dear Lord, I will remain restless, tense, and dissatisfied until I can be totally at peace in your house. But I am still on the road, still journeying, still tired and weary, and still wondering if I will ever make it to the city on the hill. With Vincent van Gogh, I keep asking your angel, whom I meet on the road: "Does the road go uphill then all the way?" And the answer is: "Yes, to the very end." And I ask again: "And will the journey take all day long?" And the answer is: "From morning till night, my friend."

So I go on, Lord, tired, often frustrated, irritated, but always hopeful to reach one day the eternal city far away, resplendent in the evening sun.

There is no certainty that my life will be any easier in the years ahead, or that my heart will be any calmer. But there is the certainty that you are waiting for me and will welcome me home when I have persevered in my long journey to your house.

O Lord, give me courage, hope, and confidence. Amen.

A CRY FOR MERCY

ITINERARY

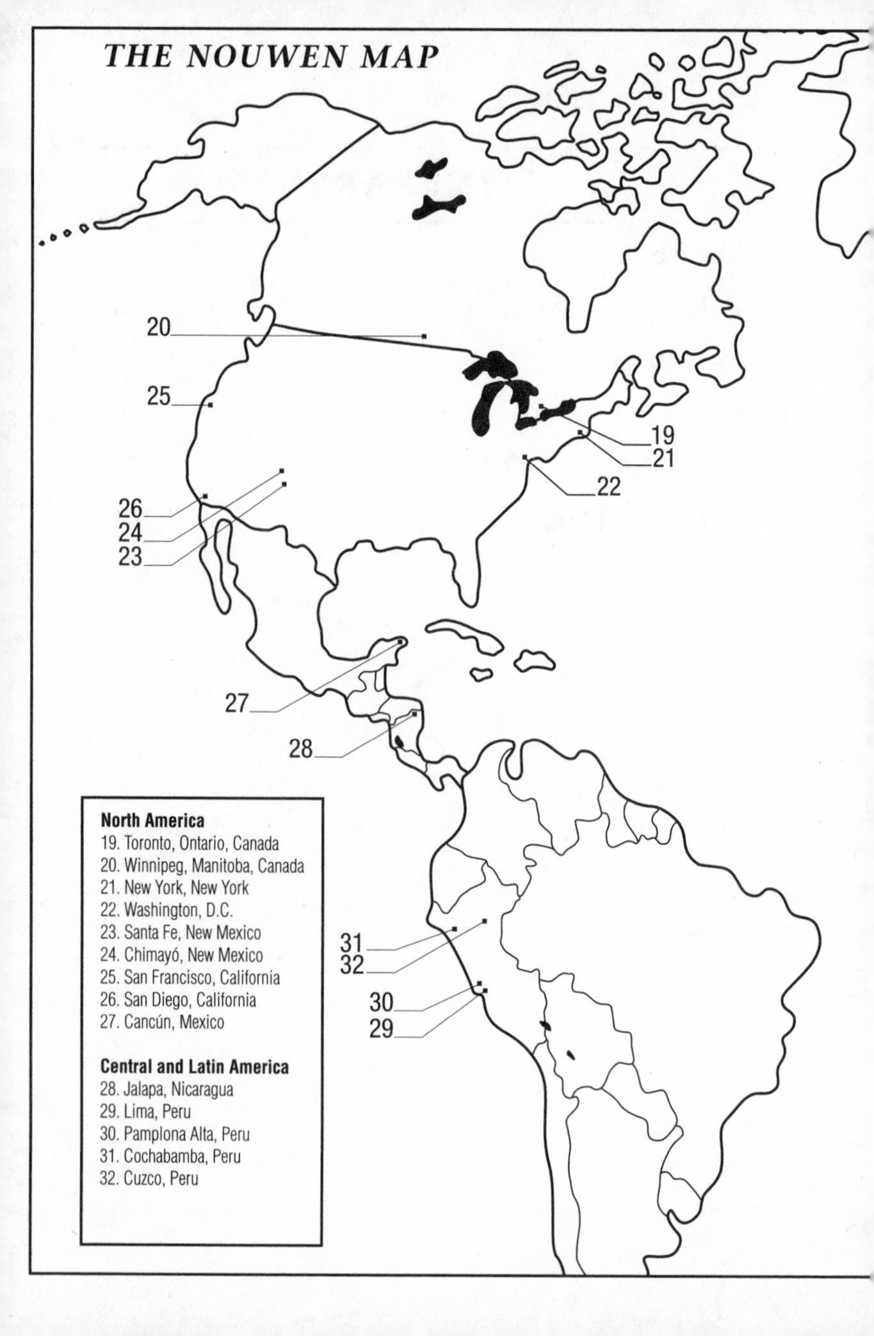
THE NOUWEN MAP
20
25
26
24
23
19
21
22
27
28
31
32
30
29
North America
19. Toronto, Ontario, Canada
20. Winnipeg, Manitoba, Canada
21. New York, New York
22. Washington, D.C.
23. Santa Fe, New Mexico
24. Chimayó, New Mexico
25. San Francisco, California
26. San Diego, California
27. Cancún, Mexico
Central and Latin America
28. Jalapa, Nicaragua
29. Lima, Peru
30. Pamplona Alta, Peru
31. Cochabamba, Peru
32. Cuzco, Peru

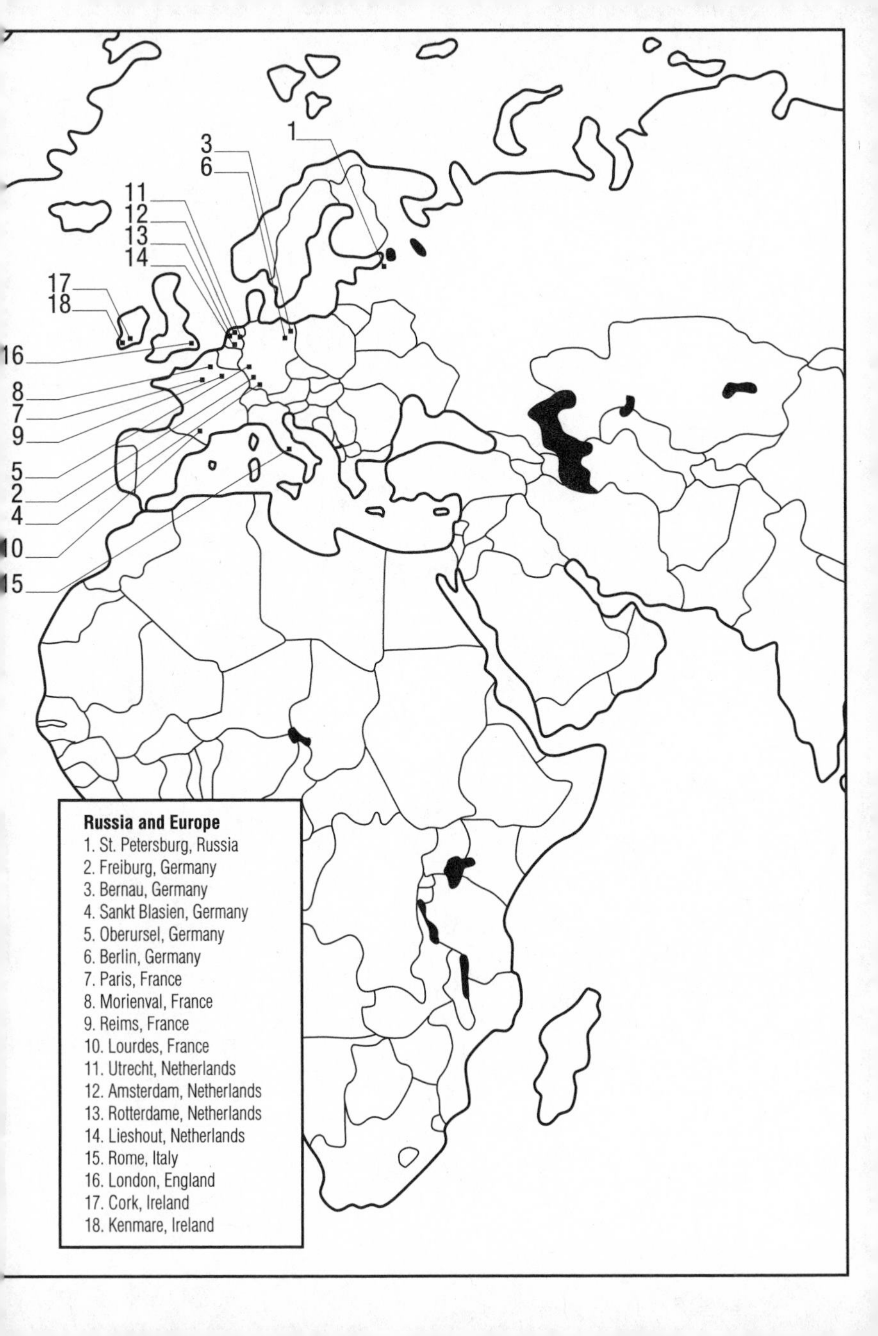
1
3
6
11
12
13
14
17
18
16
8
7
9
5
2
4
10
15
Russia and Europe
1. St. Petersburg, Russia
2. Freiburg, Germany
3. Bernau, Germany
4. Sankt Blasien, Germany
5. Oberursel, Germany
6. Berlin, Germany
7. Paris, France
8. Morienval, France
9. Reims, France
10. Lourdes, France
11. Utrecht, Netherlands
12. Amsterdam, Netherlands
13. Rotterdame, Netherlands
14. Lieshout, Netherlands
15. Rome, Italy
16. London, England
17. Cork, Ireland
18. Kenmare, Ireland

ACKNOWLEDGMENTS

A Cry for Mercy by Henri J.M. Nouwen, © 1981 by Henri J.M. Nouwen. Used by permission of Doubleday, a division of Random House, Inc.

Can You Drink the Cup? by Henri J.M. Nouwen. Copyright © 1987 by Ave Maria Press, PO Box 428, Notre Dame, IN 46556, www.avemariapress.com. Used with permission of the publisher.

"Christ of the Americas" by Henri J.M. Nouwen. America Magazine, vol. 150, issue 15, p. 293.

Clowning in Rome by Henri J.M. Nouwen © 1979 by Henri J.M. Nouwen. Used by permission of Doubleday, a division of Random House, Inc.

¡Gracias!: A Latin American Journal, Harper & Row, 1983; Orbis, 1992.

The Inner Voice of Love by Henri J.M. Nouwen, © 1996 by Henri J.M. Nouwen. Used by permission of Doubleday, a division of Random House, Inc. Also published by Darton, Longman and Todd in the United Kingdom.

Intimacy by Henri J.M. Nouwen, © 1969 by Henri J.M. Nouwen © renewed 1997 by Sue Mosteller. Reprinted by permission of HarperCollins Publishers, Inc.

Jesus and Mary: Finding Our Sacred Center © 1993 by Henri J.M. Nouwen. Used with permission of the publisher, St. Anthony Messenger Press, 28 W. Liberty St., Cincinnati, OH 45202, USA.

Making All Things New by Henri J.M. Nouwen © 1996 by Henri J.M. Nouwen. Reprinted by permission of HarperCollins Publishers, Inc.

The Return of the Prodigal Son by Henri J.M. Nouwen, © 1992 by Henri J.M. Nouwen. Used by permission of Doubleday, a division of Random House, Inc. Also published by Darton, Longman, and Todd in the United Kingdom.

The Road to Daybreak by Henri J.M. Nouwen, © 1988 by Henri J.M. Nouwen. Used by permission of Doubleday, a division of Random House, Inc. Also published as *In the House of the Lord* by Darton, Longman and Todd in the United Kingdom.

Sabbatical Journey by Henri J.M. Nouwen. Used by permission of The Crossroad Publishing Company. Also published by Darton, Longman and Todd in the United Kingdom.

The Way of the Heart by Henri J.M. Nouwen © 1981 by Henri J.M. Nouwen. Reprinted by permission of HarperCollins Publishers, Inc.

INTRODUCTION

This is a travel book with a difference.

Much has been written about the adventures of Henri J.M. Nouwen, guide of souls extraordinaire, but this is the first time he has been cast exclusively in the guise of a foreign correspondent.

Nouwen's story—Ivy League professor turned pastor among men and women with developmental disabilities—has been elaborately chronicled. For this new collection of Nouwen's writings, I have deliberately chosen to concentrate on episodes from his life which are less well known by focusing on his incidental journaling away from the familiar bases of Yale, Harvard, the Abbey of the Genesee, and L'Arche.

Some of the passages may even have been skimmed over by readers in Nouwen's many books but, plucked from their original contexts, they seem to take on a new life of their own. They bring out, in particular, the aesthetic side of his character and provide insights into how his spirituality was deepened by encounters in particular places with particular people. In these readings we meet a driven, holy man in search of the beauty of intimacy wherever he finds himself.

A sequel to my last Nouwen anthology, *The Dance of Life*, which centered on the inner pilgrimage, *A Restless Soul* charts the spiritual writer's outer meanderings. We join him beside the *Return of the Prodigal Son* in the Hermitage in St. Petersburg, observing the reconstructed world of Berlin, arguing with an astrologer in the Black Forest, admiring a work of art in the Louvre, preparing for a wedding in the beauty of Southern Ireland, attending a Mahler concert in New York, mingling with senators in Washington, listening to the stories of grieving women in Nicaragua, meeting cocaine users in a South American prison, and absorbing the majestic world of the Incas in Peru. Nouwen's world is one of striking contrasts—one minute he is rubbing shoulders with the affluent and influential, the next walking through lands of poverty and danger. But each situation tells a spiritual story and he is never slow to see the hand of God at work in the universe. His travelogue is peppered with references to sociology, history, political justice, aesthetics, psychology and, of course, theology. And throughout the restless searching, we discover a man who longs to be at rest, not by himself, but among others. Nouwen is a man of the people.

Like Nouwen, I am a restless person—the idea for this anthology emerged in a year when I found myself visiting more countries than at any other time of my life. The threat of international terrorism has, of course, made journeys through the air much less romantic than they used to be but there is still nothing like an adventure for putting you in touch with your self—and with God. Travel writing can be much more revealing than we realize. Without our firm anchors and safe havens, authors can often find themselves reflecting with greater depth than they might normally achieve from their more secure bases. And casual detail is always intriguing when we are trying to understand what makes a spiritual writer tick.

Henri Nouwen is, of course, unashamedly self-reflective in his reactions to any place he describes. The experience allows him to project his own deepest yearnings onto, for example, a canvas which then reflects back to him something about his own spiritual quest. Always conscious of the fact that his travel journals would eventually be published, Nouwen encourages his readers to open themselves to new landscapes. But, even back in 1986, it is clear from

Nouwen's pen that the nature of travel is changing dramatically:

> Traveling from Paris to Boston made me sharply aware of the contrast between the great advancements in technology and the primitive quality of human relationships. While the most sophisticated machinery took me from Paris to London in one hour and from London to Boston in six hours, the entire trip was clouded by security concerns. . . . It is obviously a good thing that so many precautions are being taken to prevent terrorist attacks, but the fact that every step of the way you are made aware that someone might try to kill you gives you a sense that the world is a precarious place to live in. The more advanced the method of transportation, the less safe it seems to be transported! Quite a few of my friends have cancelled their vacation plans because of fear of being hijacked,

bombed, or attacked on airplanes or in airports.

Technology is so far ahead of human relations! There is such a need for new ways for people to be together, to solve conflicts, to work for peace. On the level of human relations, we are still in the Stone Age, thinking that power games and fear tactics will settle our problems. Suicide attacks and military reprisals are such primitive ways to respond to threatening situations. With the technology now at hand, these primitive responses may cause the end of all human life.

More than ever it is necessary for people, who can fly to each other from faraway distances within a few hours, to speak to each other about living together in peace. Now it seems that the smaller the physical distance, the larger the moral and spiritual distance. Why do we human beings learn so much, so soon, about technology,

> and so little, so late, about loving one another? (*The Road to Daybreak*)

Henri Nouwen died as he had lived—on the move. He was traveling from Toronto in Canada to St. Petersburg in Russia to make a film when he was suddenly taken ill in his native Holland. He died a few days later of a massive heart attack. A close friend who later prayed for Nouwen beside his coffin remarked that it was the only time in her life that she had seen him still.

Traveling can take a toll on all of us, especially as we get older. After a transatlantic trip in his mid-fifties Nouwen confesses: "My long journey has harmed my prayer life. . . . I experience a certain nausea or apathy that I did not have before I left. It is a sort of spiritual fatigue, a state of lukewarmness in which I find it hard to know exactly what I feel, what I think, or what I want. It is like being a piece of driftwood on still water" (*Road to Daybreak*). But, in the years leading up to Nouwen's death, the restless lifestyle of one of the world's most influential spiritual writers began to wear him out. Friends and family warned him to take care of his body but relaxation did not come naturally to this driven man. Nouwen had always been a traveler but, during his final year, seems to have been at his most unsettled. He took a year's sabbatical but, instead of rejoicing in it as a time of rest and replenishment, he spent the entire twelve months traveling from one place to another, trekking across different continents as though desperately searching for something—or someone.

The diary of this final year, published as *Sabbatical Journey*, might leave some readers mentally exhausted as the author recounts his meanderings in relentless detail. Early in the journal he asks himself:

> Why am I so tired? Although I have all the time I want to sleep, I wake up with an immense feeling of fatigue . . . everything requires an immense effort, and after a few hours of work I collapse in utter exhaustion, often falling into a deep sleep. . . . Fatigue is a strange thing. I can push it away for a long time, I can go on automatic, especially when there are many routine things to do. But when finally the space and time are there to do something new and creative, all the repressed fatigue comes back like

> a flood and paralyses me. (*Sabbatical Journey*)

At Cancún, Mexico, in November 1995, he complains: "I am very, very tired, which is hard to explain in such a beautiful setting" (*Sabbatical Journey*). And, eight months later, in Wallenhorst, Germany, he notes: "The constant going from place to place somehow makes me lose my sense of belonging and gives me a feeling of alienation. . . . The constant fatigue makes me always look for an opportunity to sleep" (*Sabbatical Journey*). The following month, though, he is still making plans:

> A big snowstorm prevents me from leaving for Amsterdam. Just when I was all packed and ready to go, my Northwest flight was cancelled. Happily I found this out by phone so I didn't have to go to the airport. I made endless phone calls to reschedule my flight. If all goes well, I will be able to fly to Toronto tomorrow and from there to Amsterdam. But a blizzard is predicted, and my plane from Boston to Toronto might not be able to take off. Well, I hope I

> can live it patiently. I am most worried about making it to my father before Saturday since we are planning to go on vacation to Germany that day. (*Sabbatical Journey*)

So why did Nouwen keep on moving and why did he ignore advice to slow down? A clue might be found in his first book published in 1969. In *Intimacy*, he addresses the issue of depression in seminaries, pointing out that a "remarkable number" of seminarians complain about experiencing an inappropriate degree of fatigue. They sleep as long as they can, but still look tired. "Their eyelids feel heavy and they experience their bodies as something they carry around," he writes. "The philosopher might say: 'They have their bodies more than they are their bodies.' When they wake up in the morning they don't feel relaxed, but are very much aware of themselves lying on the bed as a heavy load. Even dressing becomes like a job that asks [for] concentration and special energy" (*Intimacy*).

Nearly thirty years later, while visiting Germany, Nouwen echoes those early observations: "Why can't I get rid of my fatigue? Everything exhausts me, even putting on my clothes. And everything, even seeing wonderful people and sharing wonderful meals, seems a burden or an obligation" (*Sabbatical Journey*). In the late 1960s, Nouwen had defined so-called "neurotic fatigue" as resulting from a way of living characterized by hyperawareness where people no longer rely on automatic processes, but want to know what they do from moment to moment:

> Just as a man who wants to be aware of his breathing is in danger, and one who wants to control his heartbeat cannot live, a seminarian who speaks all the time about friendship, love and community might well miss the opportunity to experience any of these realities. This lack of participating life is usually related to an often unconscious anxiety . . . his depression makes him tired, and his fatigue makes him depressed. (*Intimacy*)

Nouwen, then on the threshold of middle age, was himself always searching for "friendship, love, and community," so he would have had no difficulty in relating the restrictions of seminary life to the perimeters of his own priesthood. Like the seminarians themselves, Nouwen was no stranger to depression and the fatigue it emits. He would spend the next thirty-five years of life trying to balance travel and tiredness, a restlessness connected not only with his ongoing search for God but also with a perennial quest for personal intimacy and belonging. It is generally accepted that Nouwen carried too much "emotional baggage" around with him. This, too, was mirrored in his own traveling style. Three months before his death, he remarks:

> I keep wondering why I take so much luggage with me. I am always determined to travel light, but I always end up with more suitcases than I can carry! When I arrived at Schiphol I realized that I wouldn't be able to carry all my luggage alone. . . . At the airport, as I was going down the escalator with my loaded luggage cart, all my suitcases fell off, tumbling down the moving steps. I nearly fell over them. (*Sabbatical Journey*)

His final birthday party, organized by his sister Laurien, was celebrated with old Dutch friends in Nijmegen, Holland. "The memories that we all most had in common," he recounted, "were of our travels. Our bike trip to Belgium, our car trip to Germany, our boat trip to the island Spetsai in Greece, our plane trip to Israel, and all the events connected with these adventures" (*Sabbatical Journey*).

The underlying reasons for Nouwen's hyperactive temperament are described more fully in my biography *Wounded Prophet*. This book steps aside from the main themes of the writer's life and recreates Nouwen's travel pieces on an imaginary journey from Russia to Bolivia via Europe, Canada, and the United States of America.

The journey begins in Russia. As I explained in *Wounded Prophet*, Nouwen acknowledged the deep influence of Eastern Christian spirituality on his own life when he visited neighboring Ukraine in 1993. He wrote in his personal journal that his love of prayer, the liturgical life, and sacred art, especially icons, had all been nurtured by the Christian East. He recalled how the famous book about the Jesus Prayer, *The Way of the Pilgrim*, had made a lasting impression on him. He was captivated by the story of a simple peasant who had once walked through the country, visiting holy places in Ukraine and saying nothing but: "Lord Jesus Christ, have mercy on me." This prayer gradually "moved" from his lips to his heart until it had become one with his breathing. Wherever the peasant went, he radiated love and goodness and—to his delight—saw how people's lives changed through meeting him. Nouwen regarded it as a "charming and even humorous" eighteenth-century story that gave expression to the rich tradition of the prayer of the heart, also called the Hesychastic tradition (from the Greek, *hesychazein,* to rest).

The Hesychastic tradition found its origin in the Egyptian desert during the fourth and fifth centuries. There the desert fathers and mothers, living in the spirit of St. Anthony, said the Jesus Prayer to bring them to a complete, holy rest with God in the heart. In the sixth century, Nouwen noted, this spiritual tradition had come to full bloom in the monasteries on Mt. Sinai and, in the tenth century, on Mt. Athos in Greece. From Mt. Athos it had found its way to what today is Ukraine and Russia, and was treasured not only by monks, but also among the Orthodox laity.

The main writings of the Hesychastic tradition were compiled in the *Philokalia*. The monk, Chariton, compiled a book of excerpts which was translated into English and published under the title, *The Art of Prayer*. Few books on prayer had such a lasting influence on Nouwen than this one. His own prayer life, he admitted, had "many ups and downs" but somehow the prayer, "Lord Jesus Christ, have mercy on me," was always there—even during his driest periods. In its utter simplicity and profound compactness, it kept him connected with Jesus, especially during times when little else would. Although he lived and worshipped in the West and was daily nurtured by the Latin-rite Eucharist, his occasional contact with the Liturgy of St. John Chrysostom helped him understand more deeply about what it meant to "live in the world without being of it." He even said that participating in Eastern liturgies gave him "a sense of being in heaven before leaving earth." Here he discovered icons, not as illustrations, decorations, or ornaments, but as "true windows on the eternal."

This anthology, like many of Nouwen's books, is divided into three parts. Most of the pieces were originally composed in the places mentioned at different periods in Nouwen's life. But, as I have said, they are given fresh significance when isolated from the main body of Nouwen's work. Each page of this reconstructed travelogue is a meditation in itself. Focusing on the spirituality of people and places, these reflections put us more closely in touch with our own experiences of faith as well as offering us intriguing new insights into the heart of a one-off spiritual travel guide whose outer and inner journeys were all of a piece.

Michael Ford
in flight between London and Athens, 2007

RUSSIA AND EUROPE

St. Petersburg, Russia

Freiburg, Germany

Bernau, Germany

Sankt Blasien, Germany

Oberursel, Germany

Berlin, Germany

Paris, France

Morienval, France

Reims, France

Lourdes, France

Utrecht, Netherlands

Amsterdam, Netherlands

Rotterdam, Netherlands

Lieshout, Netherlands

Rome, Italy

London, England

Cork, Ireland

Kenmare, Ireland

LORD OF THE UNIVERSE

The Desert Fathers in their sayings point us towards a very holistic view of prayer. They pull us away from our intellectualizing practices, in which God becomes one of the many problems we have to address. They show us that real prayer penetrates to the marrow of our soul and leaves nothing untouched. The prayer of the heart is a prayer that does not allow us to limit our relationship with God to interesting words or pious emotions. By its very nature such prayer transforms our whole being into Christ precisely because it opens the eyes of our soul to the truth of ourselves as well as to the truth of God. In our heart we come to see ourselves as sinners embraced by the mercy of God. It is this vision that makes us cry out, "Lord Jesus Christ, Son of the living God, have mercy on me, a sinner." The prayer of the heart challenges us to hide absolutely nothing from God and to surrender ourselves unconditionally to his mercy.

Thus the prayer of the heart is the prayer of truth. It unmasks the many illusions about ourselves and about God and leads us into the true relationship of the sinner to the merciful God. This truth is what gives us the "rest" of the Hesychast. To the degree that this truth anchors itself in our heart, we will be less distracted by worldly thoughts and more single-mindedly directed towards the Lord of both our hearts and the universe. Thus the words of Jesus, "Happy the pure in heart: they shall see God" (Matthew 5:8), will become real in our prayer.

Temptations and struggles will remain to the end of our lives, but with a pure heart we will be restful even in the midst of a restless existence.

THE WAY OF THE HEART

A RUSSIAN MYSTIC

Hesychastic prayer, which leads to that rest where the soul can dwell with God, is prayer of the heart. For us who are so mind-oriented it is of special importance to learn to pray with and from the heart. Although they do not offer any theory about prayer, their concrete stories and counsels offer the stones with which the later orthodox spiritual writers have built a very impressive spirituality. The spiritual writers of Mount Sinai, Mount Athos, and the *startsi* of nineteenth-century Russia are all anchored in the tradition of the desert. We find the best formulation of the prayer of the heart in the words of the Russian mystic Theophan the Recluse: "To pray is to descend with the mind into the heart, and there to stand before the face of the Lord, ever-present, all-seeing, within you." All through the centuries, this view of prayer has been central in Hesychasm. Prayer is standing in the presence of God with the mind in the heart; that is, at that point of our being where there are no divisions or distinctions and where we are totally one. There God's Spirit dwells and there the great encounter takes place. There heart speaks to heart, because there we stand before the face of the Lord, all-seeing, within us.

THE WAY OF THE HEART

TOLSTOY'S MONKS

Three Russian monks lived on a faraway island. Nobody ever went there, but one day their bishop decided to make a pastoral visit. When he arrived he discovered that the monks didn't even know the Lord's Prayer. So he spent all his time and energy teaching them the "Our Father" and then left, satisfied with his pastoral work. But when his ship had left the island and was back in the open sea, he suddenly noticed the three hermits walking on the water—in fact, they were running after the ship! When they reached it they cried, "Dear Father, we have forgotten the prayer you taught us." The bishop, overwhelmed by what he was seeing and hearing, said, "But, dear brothers, how then do you pray?" They answered, "Well, we just say, 'Dear God, there are three of us and there are three of you, have mercy on us!'" The bishop, awestruck by their sanctity and simplicity, said, "Go back to your island and be at peace."

THE ROAD TO DAYBREAK

WINDOWS INTO TRANSCENDENCE

Icons are not just pious pictures to decorate churches and houses. They are images of Christ and the saints which bring us into contact with the sacred, windows that give us a glimpse of the transcendent. They need to be approached in veneration and with prayer. Only then will they reveal to us the mystery they represent.

Iconography has come to the West mainly from the Orthodox tradition, especially from Russia and Greece. Since the Russian Revolution of 1917, many Orthodox Christians have fled to the West, and through them the holy art of iconography has gradually become more known and appreciated in the Latin Church. Russian and Greek icons have become one of the most important sources of inspiration for my own prayer life. The icon of Our Lady of Vladimir, Rublev's icon of the Holy Trinity, and the nineteenth-century Greek icon of Christ that I obtained in Jerusalem have become integral parts of my life of prayer. I cannot think about the Holy Trinity, Jesus and Mary without seeing them as the holy iconographers saw them. Icons are certainly one of the most beautiful gifts of the Orthodox Church to the churches of the West.

THE ROAD TO DAYBREAK

A CIRCLE OF LOVE IN ST. PETERSBURG

Ever since becoming interested in this great work [*The Return of the Prodigal Son* painting by Rembrandt] I had known that the original had been acquired in 1766 by Catherine the Great for the Hermitage in Saint Petersburg. . . . I never dreamt that I would have a chance to see it so soon. Although I was very eager to get firsthand knowledge of a country that had so strongly influenced my thoughts, emotions, and feelings during most of my life, this became almost trivial when compared with the opportunity to sit before the painting that had revealed to me the deepest yearnings of my heart. . . . I knew that, when Rembrandt painted his *Prodigal Son,* he had lived a life that had left him with no doubt about his true and final home. I felt that, if I could meet Rembrandt right where he had painted father and son, God and humanity, compassion and misery, in one circle of love, I would come to know as much as I ever would about death and life. I also sensed the hope that through Rembrandt's masterpiece I would one day be able to express what I most wanted to say about love. . . .

And so there I was; facing the painting that had been on my mind and in my heart for nearly three years. I was stunned by its majestic beauty. Its size, larger than life; its abundant reds, browns, and yellows; its shadowy recesses and bright foreground, but most of all the light-enveloped embrace of father and son surrounded by four mysterious bystanders, all of this gripped me with an intensity far beyond my anticipation. There had been moments in which I had wondered whether the real painting might disappoint me. The opposite was true. Its grandeur and splendor made everything recede into the background and held me completely captivated.

THE RETURN OF THE PRODIGAL SON

MYSTERIOUS LIGHT BESIDE THE NEVA RIVER

While many tourist groups with their guides came and left in rapid succession, I sat on one of the red velvet chairs in front of the painting and just looked. Now I was seeing the real thing! Not only the father embracing his child-come-home, but also the elder son and the three other figures. It is a huge work in oil on canvas, eight feet high by six feet wide. It took me a while to simply *be* there, simply absorbing that I was truly in the presence of what I had so long hoped to see, simply enjoying the fact that I was all by myself sitting in the Hermitage in Saint Petersburg [beside the Neva River] looking at the *Prodigal Son* for as long as I wanted.

The painting was exposed in the most favorable way, on a wall that received plenty of natural light through a large nearby window at an eighty-degree angle. Sitting there, I realized that the light became fuller and more intense as the afternoon progressed. At four o'clock the sun covered the painting with a new brightness, and the background figures—which had remained quite vague in the early hours—seemed to step out of their dark corners. As the evening drew near, the sunlight grew more crisp and tingling. The embrace of the father and son became stronger and deeper, and the bystanders participated more directly in this mysterious event of reconciliation, forgiveness, and inner healing. Gradually I realized that there were as many paintings of the *Prodigal Son* as there were changes in the light and, for a long time, I was held spellbound by this gracious dance of nature and art.

THE RETURN OF THE PRODIGAL SON

COMIC RELIEF AT FREIBURG

A beautiful, charming, rather intimate city, built around the splendid Münster Cathedral, Freiburg sits like a precious gem in the valley between the Rhine and the first hills of the Black Forest. It is a university town, with very little industry. The centre is kept free from cars. People walk in the middle of the streets, which are lined by narrow gutters of running water. There are many beautiful churches, city gates, small medieval-looking alleys, and little squares with contemporary sculptures. It is a new city completely rebuilt after the Second World War. Yet it is a very old city rebuilt in the style and atmosphere of ages past. . . .

I have been in this country only a few times in my life and always for a very short time. The occupation of Holland during the Second World War made it hard for us to go to Germany. Somehow all my attention was directed westwards. But now I can get to know a new country, a new people, and a new way of praising God. . . . One of the stone reliefs of the Romanesque portal of the Münster . . . [which dates] from about 1210, attempts to nudge the churchgoer in a playful way towards humility. A king is seated in a small basket which is hanging by a cord bound on both ends to the necks of two huge birds. The king holds in his hands two long spits on which two rabbits are impaled. By trying to reach the rabbits with their beaks, the hungry birds lift up the king into the air.

This comic relief portrays the story of Alexander the Great who, after having conquered the whole world, also tries to make it to heaven. Although different versions of the story exist, one of them says that when Alexander saw the earth beneath him as a small hat in a large sea, he realized how tiny the world really is and how ridiculous it had been to spend his life trying to conquer it. Thus Alexander is presented to the pious churchgoer as an example of silly pride.

Konrad Kunze, the author of a beautiful book about the Münster, entitled *Heaven in Stone*, summarizes a sermon of Berthold von Regensburg given around 1260: "Alexander, for whom the world was too small, becomes in the end only seven feet of dust, just like the poorest man ever born; Alexander thought that he could pull down the highest stars from heaven with his hands. And you, as he, would love to go up in the air, if you could only do it. But the story of Alexander shows the result of such high flying and proves that the great Alexander was one of the greatest fools the world has ever seen."

Well, no subtleties here! I wonder what Berthold would have thought about Boeing 747s. Still . . . the Münster itself, with its high-rising Gothic arches, might prove to be as much a sign of civic pride as of humility in the eyes of God. People always had mixed motives! God have mercy on us.

THE ROAD TO DAYBREAK

THE MEDIEVAL TOUR GUIDE

This afternoon I went downtown to pay another visit to the Münster. Together with a middle-aged woman, I took a guided tour. It was a wonderful experience. The guide, a retired civil servant, not only told us the history of the church, the names of the architects and artists, and the meaning of the statues, paintings and altars, he also viewed the tour as an occasion to preach. He saw it as his task to convert us and bring us to prayer.

As he showed us the majestic portal on which both the saved and the condemned are vividly portrayed, he said, "Let us pray that we end up in the right group." As he showed us a large tapestry of

Melchizedek, he recounted elaborately the Old Testament story and its eucharistic application. As he explained the New Testament scenes portrayed in stone or glass or on canvas, he quoted long passages from the Gospels by heart. In between the art treasures he demonstrated to us the ugly wooden contemporary confessionals with lights to indicate if they are free or occupied, and exhorted us to go to confession at least once every two weeks. . . .

As we walked through the huge central nave, our guide spotted a young man with a cap on his head. The guide told him without subtlety that this was God's house and that he had to remove his cap or leave. The man left, rather perplexed about the encounter. I was shocked by this confronting, pious, nationalistic, and very moralistic guide. It struck me that the man fits the Münster perfectly. His way of guiding reveals both its greatness and its medieval, clerical and authoritarian qualities. But what about the young man who was sent away? Would he ever be able to come back and discover the gentle all-forgiving love of God?

THE ROAD TO DAYBREAK

THE REFLECTIVE HEIDEGGER

Freiburg is the city of Martin Heidegger (1889–1976). Shortly after I arrived here, Franz Johna drove me past 47 Rötebuckweg, where Heidegger lived and wrote many of his philosophical works.

There are few philosophers who have had as much influence on my thinking as Martin Heidegger. Though I never studied Heidegger directly, many of the philosophers, psychologists, and theologians who formed my thinking were deeply influenced by him. Walgrave, Binswanger, and Rahner cannot be fully understood apart from Heidegger's existentialism.

Today I read a short address given in 1955 in Messkirch, his birthplace, in honor of the musician Conrad Kreutzer, who was also born there. The address is entitled "Gelassenheit." Heidegger states that the greatest danger of our time is that the calculating way of thinking, that is part of the technical revolution, will become the dominating and exclusive way of thinking. Why is this so dangerous?

Heidegger says, "Because then we would find, together with the highest and the most successful development of our thinking on the calculating level, an indifference towards reflection and a complete thoughtlessness . . . then humanity would have renounced and thrown away what is most its own, its ability to reflect. What is at stake is to save the essence of humanity. What is at stake is to keep alive our reflective thinking (*das Nachdenken*)."

Heidegger calls for an attitude in which we say "yes" to the new techniques, insofar as they serve our daily lives, and "no" when they claim our whole being. He calls for a *Gelassenheit zu Dingen* (letting reality speak) and an openness to the mystery of things. This calmness and openness, Heidegger says, will give us a new rootedness, a new groundedness, a new sense of belonging. Thus we can remain reflective human beings and prevent ourselves from becoming victims of a "calculating" existence.

It is clear how important Heidegger's thoughts remain today. We need to safeguard our reflective minds more than ever. Indirectly, Heidegger also touches on the need for a new spirituality, a new way of being in the world, without being of it.

THE ROAD TO DAYBREAK

CARNIVAL MASKS AND SERIOUS FACES

Rosenmontag (Carnival's Monday) in Freiburg. At 2 p.m. I went downtown for the carnival parade and saw clowns, bands, small and large floats, an endless variety of masks, and an abundance of confetti. It was bitterly cold. People kept themselves warm with waffles and *Gluhwein* (hot spiced wine). The parade numbered 149 shows, and it took two hours to pass.

Most impressive were the huge masks. They were often pieces of art expressing a variety of emotions: anger, joy, hatred, love, goodness, and evil. Some masks were so realistic I could hardly imagine that the people wearing them had a different feeling from what the mask expressed.

Some heads were so huge that their wearers' faces could be seen only through windows in the neck. Many blew trumpets, flutes, or horns through the windows. I was struck by the contrast between the faces on the masks and the faces in the windows. The "window faces" all looked quite serious, compared to the wild faces on the heads above them. While the parade invited us to be fools for the day, it convinced me how hard it is for people to relax and truly celebrate. Also, the people on the sidewalks watching the parade took it all in with great seriousness. If there had not been so many bands, it would have been an extremely dull event. It all had a somewhat obligatory quality. Even wildly dressed people had a hard time smiling! It was a serious job for them. The children seemed the most serious of all. Whether they looked like cats, mice, polar bears, screwdrivers, Indians, Mexicans, or witches, their little faces showed that they were performing an important task!

I watched all this, ate a waffle, drank two cups of *Gluhwein* and went home. The [Vincentian] sister who opened the door greeted me with an open face, a big smile, and a free laugh. I suddenly realized that no mask can make people really happy. Happiness must come from within.

THE ROAD TO DAYBREAK

CONSOLATION AT DUSK

Saturday afternoon, 5 p.m. at the Münster. It is very still on the Münster square. A very light, hardly noticeable, snow falls on the cobblestones. The houses standing around the Münster form a quiet, peaceful community, like children sitting around a bonfire listening to a story. There is hardly any noise. The stores have been closed since noon. No cars, no shouting voices, not even the noise of children playing. Here and there I see people crossing the empty snow-covered square and entering the church. The sun has gone down, but it is not fully dark yet. The grey sky is filled with little white dots. A few lights burn outside guesthouses, inviting people to come in and drink some wine or eat some hearty food.

I look up at the tower of the Münster. She tells her story without words, a wise old grandmother smiling at her children, who say "Tell us that story again." Beams of light cover her full length and, through the open spire, a warm inner light shines forth from her. I look and feel comforted and consoled. She seems to say, "Do not worry so much. God loves you."

In the church it is dark. But there is an island of light in front of the large statue of the Virgin and Child. The flames of hundreds of small candles make the light look like something alive and moving. A few people are standing there praying with closed eyes.

In the little side chapels, surrounding the main altar, priests are hearing confessions. People come and go silently. I kneel in front of one of the priests to confess my sins. He listens to me attentively and speaks gentle words about the importance of being joyful at all times. As he absolves me in the name of the Father, the Son, and the Holy Spirit, I feel some of the joy he spoke about.

I pray for a while in front of the statue of the Virgin. Then I walk home with a heart full of peace. It has become very dark now. The glowing tower still stands there and smiles at me. All is well.

THE ROAD TO DAYBREAK

AN ASTROLOGER IN THE BLACK FOREST

Today Franz took us on a little trip to Bernau, known for its wood-carving workshops, and to Sankt Blasien, known for its high-domed church. Most beautiful, however, was the trip itself, through the snow-covered Black Forest. It felt like driving through a very romantic Christmas card. The view into the valleys with their little villages and charming church towers, the winding roads, the white and green fir trees, and the heavy clouds moving between the hills and mountains was so pleasant to the eye from a well-heated Mercedes.

What I will probably most remember of our trip was a woman called Ursula. She was sitting alone in the restaurant where we went for lunch. When she noticed us, she offered us a glass of red wine. I accepted her offer and, as a result she joined us a little later, obviously in need of company. Ursula is an astrologer who tried to convince us of the importance of her gifts to determine our personalities on the basis of the year, the day, and the minute of our birth. She spoke intensely, intrusively, and hardly gave us a chance to respond.

Soon she was busy attacking the Vatican, calling the Pope a poisonous influence, and telling us that she believed in God but had no use whatsoever for the church. She also declared that all the good Popes had been murdered, John Paul I being one of them, that the crusades, Inquisition, and pogroms showed how evil the church is, that Leonardo Boff was her hero, and that most theologians didn't know what they were talking about.

After listening to her tirade for ten minutes, I felt an unusually strong desire to put a needle in her balloon. So I looked her straight in the eyes, asked her to listen to me for a change, and told her that

I was a Catholic priest, worked with handicapped people, had met the Pope himself, knew all about Leonardo Boff, and considered her tirade insensitive, simplistic, trendy, and very arrogant. I went on to say to her, "You are a person who has influence on people. What you say is important. Please mind that your words don't wound those you speak with, and please realize that the history of Christianity cannot be summarized in two or three condemnations."

Ursula fell completely silent. She hadn't expected such a strong response. She accepted my words as well as she could, asked me for my name, and wrote her name down for me. I am not sure if I did the right thing. Franz said, "I never heard you defend the Pope in such an unconditional way." I realized that Ursula's simplistic criticism of the church had made me a somewhat simplistic supporter. I don't think I was able to change her mind, but she certainly made me aware of my own mind!

SABBATICAL JOURNEY

BODY AND SPIRIT AT THE CIRCUS

At 2:00 p.m. I had a fast and easy train ride to Oberursel [Germany], where Rodleigh was waiting.

. . . It was good to see the Flying Rodleighs again. They were in good spirits and happy with the new shape of their trapeze act. . . . Every new place requires a careful checking of distances, floor level, heights, and many other details. A trapeze act is such precision work that small irregularities in the rigging can be fatal.

I am suddenly aware of how intimate the circus tent is. Last year and the year before I saw the Rodleighs performing in halls in Rotterdam and Zwolle that could seat sixty thousand people or more. There the trapeze act took place at a great distance and lost some of its warmth. Now I can see it in its normal surroundings.

The 3:30 p.m. show brought in hundreds of children. I hadn't expected that I would be so moved seeing the Rodleighs again, but I found myself crying as I watched them flying and catching under the big top. . . . The choreography was elegant; there were many wonderful surprises, and the whole performance felt very energetic. Even though I have seen the Flying Rodleighs for five years now and have attended dozens of their shows, they never bore me. There always seems to be something new, something original, something fresh. . . .

As I watched them in the air, I felt some of the same emotion as when I saw them for the first time with my father in 1991. It is hard to describe, but it is the emotion coming from the experience of an enfleshed spirituality. Body and spirit are fully united. The body in its beauty and elegance expresses the spirit of love, friendship, family, and community, and the spirit never leaves the here and now of the body.

. . . Tonight I saw the show again. I was fascinated by a pair of blood brothers who performed a quite amazing contortionist act. The way they folded their bodies and wrapped themselves around each other created a feeling that these brothers are the most intimate of friends. But I heard after the show that they do not like each other, they live in separate trailers, they talk to each other only about work; and they are in competition about who is the best. It is so sad that people who act out brotherhood, friendship, and intimacy live the opposite.

. . . At the end of the practice session Rodleigh asked me if I would like to make a swing or two. I said, "Sure, I'd love to." First he helped me get into the net and showed me how to climb the long ladder to the pedestal. It is an intimidating place to be. The space below, above, and around me felt enormous and awesome. Kerri and Slava pulled me up onto the pedestal, put the safety belt around me, held me tight, and handed me the bar. As I held the bar I wondered if I would be able to hold my own weight, but when they pushed me off I felt at ease swinging above the net a few times. I tried to kick a little to get higher but simply didn't have much breath left, so Rodleigh told me how to drop into the net. I repeated the whole sequence once more with a tiny bit more grace. Then Rodleigh agreed to give me a sense of the catcher's grip. So I climbed the ladder on the catcher's side, and Jonathon, who was hanging head down on the catchbar, grabbed me by my wrists and held me hanging there for a while. I looked up into his upside-down face and could imagine how it would be to swing while being held by him. Altogether I was happy with the experience. It got me as close as I will ever come to being a trapeze artist!

SABBATICAL JOURNEY

ABSENCE AND PRESENCE

Today I had a very long train ride. My friend, Tom Day, was on the platform at the Berlin station. . . . As Tom and I traveled by subway and car to

Tom's home, he told me about his son's sudden and tragic death at his university. What incredible grief. A brilliant life cut short. When we got to the house, Helga was there to welcome us. I can hardly believe how they are surviving this enormous tragedy. Their son, Lars, the pride and joy of their lives, had died suddenly and totally unexpectedly.

. . . After breakfast and the Eucharist, Tom and Helga took me on a tour of Berlin. Visiting Berlin is quite an emotional experience for me. There are many familiar names and images: Brandenburger Tor, the Reichstag, Unter den Linden, and so on. But seeing these things all at once in their natural setting and hearing Tom and Helga speak about them was like seeing my own life from a new perspective. The end of the Weimar Republic, the burning of the Reichstag, Hitler's coming to power, the Second World War and the hatred of Jews; the Russian invasion of Berlin and the destruction of the city; the Allied control of the city in three sectors; the division into East and West Berlin; the building of the Berlin Wall in 1961, and John F. Kennedy's words "Ich bin ein Berliner" (I am a Berliner) in 1963; the taking down of the wall and the end of Communism; the decision in 1990 to make Berlin the centre of the German government again; and the total rebuilding of the city. All of these events I lived from a distance, and many of them I remember as significant moments of my life. Now I could see it all in stone and live it all again within a few hours.

It was history coming alive. I deeply feel my own responsibility. It *does* make a difference how I live my life. It *does* make a difference where I go, with whom I speak, and what I write. Yes, my life is very short and seems so insignificant in the context of our immense universe. But seeing what I saw today and hearing what I heard today, I experience a great desire to live with as much integrity, as much clarity, and as much courage as I can.

All through the day we talked about Tom and Helga's son. He was very present and very absent. It feels as if I came just too late to meet an exceptionally beautiful young man, full of life, full of love, and full of hope. With enormous pain, I feel some of it in my own heart. I cannot even fathom what Tom and Helga were feeling as they showed me this city, and as we walked and talked together.

SABBATICAL JOURNEY

SILENT ADORATION IN PARIS

Today I went to the Louvre in Paris with Brad Wolcott to see Rembrandt's *The Pilgrims of Emmaus*. . . .

At first sight, the painting was a disappointment. It was much smaller than I had expected and surrounded by so many other paintings that it was hard to see it as a separate work of art. Maybe I was too familiar with it through reproductions to be genuinely surprised. Brad and I stood in front of it just looking at the event portrayed.

Jesus sits behind the table looking up in prayer while holding a loaf of bread in his hands. On his right, one of the pilgrims leans backwards with his hands folded; while on his left, the other has moved his chair away from the table and gazes with utter attention at Jesus. Behind him a humble servant, obviously unaware of what is happening, reaches forward to put a plate of food on the table. On the table, a bright white cloth only partially covers the heavy table rug. There are very few objects on the table: three pewter plates, a knife, and two small cups. Jesus sits in front of a majestic stone apse flanked by two big, square pillars. On the right side of the painting, the entrance door is visible, and there is a coat stand in the corner over which a cape has been casually thrown. In the left corner of the room, a doglike figure can be seen lying under a bench. The whole painting is in endless varieties of brown: light brown, dark brown, yellow-brown, red-brown, and so on. The source of light is not revealed, but the white tablecloth is the brightest part of the painting.

Brad and I noticed that the bare feet of Jesus and the two pilgrims were painted with great detail. Not so the feet of the servant. Rembrandt obviously wanted us to know about the long tiring walk they had just made. The large door and the cape on the coat stand were also there to remind us of the journey. These men truly came from somewhere.

As we looked at the painting, many people passed by. One of the guides said, "Look at Jesus' face, in ecstasy, yet so humble." That expressed beautifully what we saw. Jesus' face is full of light, a light which radiates from his head in a cloudlike halo. He does not look at the men around him. His eyes look upward in an expression of intimate communion with the Father. While Jesus is in deep prayer, he yet remains present; he remains the humble servant who came to be among us and show us the way to God.

The longer we looked at the painting, the more we felt drawn into the mystery it expresses. We gradually came to realize that the unoccupied side of the table across from Jesus is the place for the viewers. Brad said, "Now I see that Rembrandt painted the Eucharist, a sacramental event to which we, as we view it, are invited." It suddenly dawned on me how many similarities exist between this painting and Rublev's Trinity icon. There, as here, the white table is the real centre. There, as here, the viewer is made a real part of the mystery of the Eucharist. As we continued to let the painting speak to us, we were amazed that we both came to see it more and more as a call to worship Christ in the Eucharist. The hands of Jesus holding the bread on the white altar table are the centre, not only of the light, but also of the sacramental action. Yet if Jesus were to leave the altar, the bread would still be there. And we would still be able to be with him.

For an instant the museum became a church, the painting a sanctuary, and Rembrandt a priest. All of it told me something about God's hidden presence in the world. When we walked away from the painting and merged with the crowd of tourists headed for the *Mona Lisa* and the *Venus de Milo*, we felt as if we were returning to a busy street after a time of silent adoration in a holy place.

THE ROAD TO DAYBREAK

PARISIAN LIFE

As Peter and I walked through Paris today, we were impressed by its abundance as well as by its poverty. The stores, be they bookstores or food-stores, offer a wealth and variety found in few other cities. People throng the city, looking, buying, drinking coffee, having lively conversations, laughing, kissing, and playing.

In the subways, guitarists and singers with portable microphones and loudspeakers join the ride, sing rock songs, and ask for donations. On the train we were treated to a puppet show with a dancing moon, a talking bear, and a sweet melody.

Paris is full of life, movement, art, music, and people of all ages, races, and nationalities. So much is going on—often at the same time—that it is hard not to feel overwhelmed by the enormous variety of impressions. Paris is exhilarating, surprising, exciting, and stimulating, but also very tiring.

We also saw the other side: many poor, hungry people living on the streets, sleeping in subway stations, sitting on church steps, begging for money. There are so many unemployed, so many alcoholics, so many drug users, so many mentally and physically ill people that those who want to offer them shelter, food, and counsel can never feel they have finished the task. Amid all the beauty, wealth, and abundance of Paris, there is immense suffering, undeniable loneliness, and unreachable human anguish.

THE ROAD TO DAYBREAK

CÉZANNE THE MYSTIC

Just a week after I had bought some postcards with reproductions of paintings by Cézanne, Rainer Maria Rilke's *Letters on Cézanne* was sent to me as a Christmas gift. It is a happy coincidence. Ever since I read *Letters to a Young Poet,* I have felt a deep connection with Rilke. Now he will introduce me to Cézanne, whose paintings I like but have not yet fully seen. Rilke will help me to see.

When Rilke wrote to his wife, Clara, about Cézanne's painting of Mont Sainte-Victoire, he said: "Not since Moses has anyone seen a mountain so greatly . . . only a saint could be as united with his God as Cézanne was with his work." For Rilke, Cézanne was indeed a mystic who helped us to see reality in a new way. He writes about Cézanne as a painter who "so incorruptibly reduced a reality to its color content that that reality resumed a new existence in a beyond of color, without any previous memories."

Cézanne, in Rilke's view, was able to be fully present to the present and could therefore see reality as it is. This was also Rilke's own desire. He suffered from his inability to be fully in the present and thus see clearly. He writes, "One lives so badly, because one always comes into the present unfinished, unable, distracted. . . ."

Cézanne's paintings revealed to Rilke a man able to live . . . totally present to the present, truly seeing. This was Rilke's own search.

I am so glad for this encounter with Rilke and Cézanne because they both bring me closer to the place where true living and true seeing are one.

THE ROAD TO DAYBREAK

THE MONASTIC OASIS OF ST. GERVAIS

Tonight we attended Vespers and Mass at the Church of St. Gervais [Paris], undoubtedly one of the most remarkable centers of new religious vitality in France.

St. Gervais is the spiritual home of the Monastic Fraternities of Jerusalem. These parallel communities of men and women have chosen the city as their place of prayer, in contrast to the great contemplative orders of the past, which built their monasteries and abbeys in the peaceful countryside.

Being in St. Gervais and praying with the monks and nuns—and the several hundred Parisians who had come directly from their work to the service—was a deeply moving experience for Peter and me. The liturgy was both festive and solemn, a real expression of adoration. The monks and nuns wore flowing white robes. The music had a prayerful, polyphonic quality, reminiscent of Byzantine rites. There were icons, candles, and incense. People sat on the floor or on small benches. The atmosphere was very quiet, harmonious, prayerful, and peaceful. To come from the busy, restless city streets into the large church, and to be embraced by the simple splendor of the liturgy, was an experience that made a deep impression on both of us.

Peter picked up a flyer describing the spirituality of the brothers and sisters of Jerusalem. There I read:

> Life in the city today is a wilderness for the masses of men and women who live alone, some worrying about the future, some unconcerned, each unknown to the other. The brothers and sisters of Jerusalem want to live in solidarity with them, just as they are now, and wherever they are. They wish to provide them with some kind of oasis, freely open to all, a silent place alive with prayer, in a spirit of welcome and sharing, where real life means more than mere talking and acting. A peaceful place where all people, whatever their social background, their age, or their outlook on life, are invited to come and share in a common search for God.

At St. Gervais, we found what these words describe. I have often thought about the possibility of living a truly contemplative life in the heart of the city. Is it possible? Or just a romantic dream? At Cambridge [Massachusetts] I had tried to start something like that among my students. But my own busyness, restlessness, and inner tension showed that I was not yet ready for it.

THE ROAD TO DAYBREAK

GOTHIC VESPERS AT MORIENVAL

This afternoon Peter and I attended Vespers in the church of Our Lady of Morienval. Morienval is a small village about a half hour's drive from Trosly [in northern France].

We were not prepared for this unusual event. About thirty people sang Vespers together for the first Sunday of Advent. Most of them were members of religious orders from the area. The pastor who had organized the simple service told us that no vespers had been sung in that church since 1745, when the Benedictine sisters, whose abbey church it was, left the area. It was a moving experience to pray with this small group of believers. We reached out over the centuries to those who had preceded us and took up the prayer that had been interrupted for 240 years.

This in itself was unusual enough. But when the service was over and we had a chance to look around, we realized that we had come upon one of the most precious architectural gems in France. Built around 1050 in fine Romanesque style, the church has a central nave, three aisles, and a majestic clock tower. Its wide transepts and semicircular choir are flanked by two elegant, decorative towers. Compared to a cathedral, it is a small, homely church. We were astonished to see an eleventh-century church in such a fine state of preservation. Neither the feudal conflicts of the Middle Ages, not the French Revolution, nor the First and Second World Wars had done any harm to it. It is undoubtedly one of the best preserved Romanesque churches in France.

The pastor of the church was eager to tell us about its history. He took us to the apse and showed us that one of the arches was pointed, in contrast to the rounded curves of the other Romanesque arches. As if he were betraying a secret, he whispered, "It is said that this is the first Gothic arch in the world." I was quite impressed to stand at the birthplace of the Gothic style, which would dominate the next several centuries. As a whole, the church was still round, down-to-earth, and simple. But the builder had begun to express an urge to go higher and strive for the heavens!

The pastor turned on all the lights in the church and let the tower bells ring. Suddenly all was light and sound. We felt privileged to have a glimpse of the devotion and faith of people who had lived nine hundred years before us. They sang with the same psalms as we did and prayed to the same Lord as we did. We felt once again a joyful, hope-giving connection with the past.

THE ROAD TO DAYBREAK

MAJESTY AND HUMILITY AT REIMS

So here we are in Reims in the convent of the Sisters of St. Claire. It is a space filled with silence, prayer, and contemplation. Through the window of my room I see in the distance the majestic Cathedral of Notre Dame rising up the centre of the city. . . .

In the convent where we are staying there is a small prayer room. It is decorated with a simple stained-glass window representing the burning bush, a wooden pillar in which a small tabernacle is carved, some prayer stools and benches, and some small lamps attached to the bamboo-covered walls.

Nathan and I prayed our psalms there and spent some time in silence. It felt very peaceful and restful. Hardly any sounds could be heard.

In the afternoon we went to downtown Reims to visit the Cathedral of Notre Dame. Coming from the small prayer chapel into the majestic nave of the cathedral felt like touching the two extremes of the presence of God in our world. God's hiddenness and God's splendor, God's smallness and God's majesty, God's silence and God's creative word, God's humility and God's triumphant glory. Here in this sacred space, built in the thirteenth century, the Saint-King Louis was consecrated (1226), Jeanne d'Arc attended the coronation of Charles VII (1429), Charles X was crowned (1825), and Charles de Gaulle and Konrad Adenauer celebrated the reconciliation between the French and the Germans (1962). So many emotions and feelings, so many tragic and joyous events, so many ugly and beautiful memories, so much pride and so much faith, so much desire for power and so much—simple faith.

During World War I, much of the cathedral was burned and destroyed. But in 1937, after twenty years of restoration, it was reopened and reconsecrated by Cardinal Suhard, and today visitors come and gaze at its splendor. After some time trying to absorb some of the cathedral's majesty, Nathan and I sat at a little terrace on the cathedral square and just looked at the three saint-filled entrance portals, at the rosette, at the statues of kings and bishops, and at the two massive towers.

THE ROAD TO DAYBREAK

THE POVERTY OF LOURDES

There are very few pilgrims at this time of the year. I am here alone. After the long, tiring night on the train, I arrived at "the little convent" of the Sisters of the Immaculate Conception at 7:30 a.m. I slept, went to the grotto where Mary appeared to Bernadette, celebrated the Eucharist of the Epiphany in the basilica and prayed. Why am I here? To give my life to Jesus. To make Jesus the very centre of my existence. But how is this to come about? Mary is here to show me. Mary is here to be my gentle counselor, to take me by the hand and let me enter into full communion with her son.

I am afraid, but Mary is here and tells me to trust. I realize that I can make Jesus the heart of my heart only when I ask Mary to show me how. She is the mother of Jesus. In her, God interrupted history and started to make everything new.

. . . Today is the feast of the Baptism of Jesus, a dark and rainy day. At the grotto, everything speaks of water: the rushing Gave River, the drizzling rain from the cloudy sky, the spring of Masabielle. . . . The large space before the grotto is empty. Here and there I see people with umbrellas walking close to the place where Mary spoke to Bernadette. They touch the rocks forming the cave, watch the little spring, let their rosaries move through their fingers, look up to the statue of Mary, make the sign of the cross and light a candle. It is grey, cold, damp, and empty. No music, no songs, no processions.

I want to be purified. I want to be cleansed. I go to the baths. There, two men instruct me to undress. They wrap a blue apron around my waist, ask me to concentrate on what intercessions I want to ask of Mary, then lead me into the bath and immerse me in the ice-cold water. When I stand again, they pray the Hail Mary with me and give me a cup of water from the spring to drink. There are no towels with which to dry myself. And so, shivering and wet, I put my clothes back on, go back to the grotto and pray. . . .

On this dark, rainy day there is little to please the senses: no sun, no foliage, no candlelight. Under little tin-roofed stalls, some men are burning candles in bunches of hundreds, but it doesn't warm my heart. Everything comes back to the basic questions: "Do you want to see? Do you want to let go of your sin? Do you want to repent?" I do, I do, but I do not know how to make it happen.

I walk from the grotto to the basilica above it. Many steps lead me to the little square overlooking the valley of the Gave. Entering the crypt of the church, where the Blessed Sacrament is adored during the day, I see the host enclosed in a large glass triangle held up by a tree-like structure. A few people are praying. It is very quiet. I sit down before the altar on which the Blessed Sacrament rests.

After an hour, I sense a deep need of forgiveness and healing. I go to a priest in the chapel of confessions across the way from the basilica. He speaks to me for a long time. His French is difficult for me to understand. I strain to listen. He mentions the poverty of Lourdes in January and says, "It is good for you to be here now. Pray to Mary and Bernadette and be willing to let go of the old and let God's grace touch you as it touched Mary and Bernadette. Don't be afraid to be poor, alone, naked, stripped of all your familiar ways of doing things. God is not finished with you yet." He absolves me of all my sins and tells me to say a prayer that reminds me that

I belong to God. I shake hands with this stranger-friend and I feel a little lighter.

JESUS AND MARY: FINDING OUR SACRED CENTER

STRANGER IN THE NETHERLANDS

Early this morning I walked around Utrecht trying to find a church where I could go to pray. But the two churches I came upon were closed and, when I rang the rectory doorbell, there was no response. As I walked through the streets saying the rosary, I felt like a stranger among my own people.

Later I took a train to Amsterdam to visit a friend, and from there I went to Rotterdam to celebrate New Year's Eve with my brother and his family. At 7 p.m. I celebrated the Eucharist in the nearby parish church. My little six-year-old niece was willing to go with me, but everyone else preferred to stay home. Except for the sacristan, little Sarah, and myself, there was nobody in the big old church. I felt lonely, especially because I couldn't share God's gifts with those who are closest to me. My deepest thoughts and feelings have become foreign to them. . . .

It has become a sort of tradition that I celebrate the Eucharist on the first day of the year with the Van Campen family in Lieshout, near Eindhoven. . . . For me it is an annual confrontation with the tragedy of Dutch Catholicism. Phillip and his wife, Puck, are both deeply believing people. Their life centers around the Eucharist. Puck, whose days are fully dedicated to the care of her invalid husband, continues to find hope and strength in Jesus through his presence in her life. But for the children the words "God" and "Church" have become much more ambiguous and often evoke very critical and sometimes even hostile thoughts. The two older sons and their families still visit the church regularly. They see the life in Christ as important but often wonder if the services they attend really nurture their spiritual life. The younger children, however, have become much more alienated. For them, the Church has become irrelevant. For most of them the Bible is no longer used, the sacraments have become unknown, prayer is nonexistent, and thoughts about a greater life than the present are rather utopian.

The grandchildren seem most ill at ease with religious ceremonies. Six of them have not been baptized and look at me, vested in alb and stole, as some performer who is not very entertaining.

It was quite an experience to pray and celebrate the Eucharist surrounded by a large family in which the parents are deeply committed Christians, the children find themselves less and less at home in the Church, and most of the grandchildren have become unfamiliar with the story of God's love.

All of these men and women are very good, caring, and responsible people. Their friendship means a lot to me and gives me joy. Still, I experience a real sadness that the faith that gives so much life to the parents no longer shapes the lives of all the children and grandchildren. Who is to blame? I often wonder where I would be today if I had been part of the great turmoil of the Dutch Church during the last decades. Blaming is not the issue. What is important is to find the anger-free parts in people's hearts where God's love can be heard and received.

THE ROAD TO DAYBREAK

THE DEEPER CONNECTION

I spent most of the afternoon with one of my best Dutch friends and his family. . . . We spoke about the existential loneliness we are both experiencing at this time in our lives. This loneliness stems not from a lack of friends, problems with spouse or children, or absence of professional recognition. Neither of us has any major complaints in these areas. Still . . . the question "What am I doing, and for what reason?" lurks underneath all of our good feelings about friends, family, and work. Wim spoke about experiences of "de-realization" which are "beyond psychological explanation." As we have both passed fifty, we have discovered that at times we look at our world with a strange inner question: "What am I doing here? Is this really our world, our people, our existence? What is everybody so busy with?"

This question comes from a place deeper than emotions, feelings, or passions. It is a question about the meaning of existence, raised not just by the mind, but also by a searching heart, a question which makes us feel like strangers in our own milieu. People take on a robotlike quality. They do many things but don't seem to have an interior life. Some outside power seems to "wind them up" and make them do whatever they are doing. This "de-realization" experience is extremely painful, but it can also be the way to a deeper connection.

Wim and I spoke about this deeper connection. Without a deep-rooted sense of belonging, all of life can easily become cold, distant, and painfully repetitive. This deeper connection is the connection with the one whose name is love, leading to a new discovery that we are born out of love and are always called back to that love. It leads to a new realization that God is the God of life who continues to offer us life wherever and whenever death threatens. It ultimately leads to prayer. And from our being human, being child, brother or sister, father or mother, grandfather or grandmother comes a new experience of being held within the hand of a loving God.

THE ROAD TO DAYBREAK

FACES OF LOVE IN ROME

It took a while to get used to living in a building overlooking the Vatican as well as the monument of Victor Emmanuel; it took a while to become familiar with both the solemnity of the papal ceremonies in St. Peter's and the fervor of the demonstrations in Piazza Venezia; it took a while to feel at home in a city in which piety and violence rival each other in their intensity; and it took a while to take for granted that the devout worshippers in Piazza San Pietro are as much part of Roman life as the bohemians on Piazza

Navona. But after a month, the imposing buildings, the large crowds, and the sensational events seemed little more than the milieu for something much less visible but much more penetrating.

During these five months in Rome it wasn't the red cardinals or the Red Brigade who had the most impact on me, but the little things that took place between the great scenes. I met a few students of the San Egidio community "wasting" their time with grade-school dropouts and the elderly. I met a Medical Mission sister dedicating all her time to two old women who had become helpless and isolated in their upstairs rooms in Trastevere. I met young men and women picking up the drunks from the streets during the night and giving them a bed and some food.

I met a priest forming communities for the handicapped. I met a monk who with three young Americans had started a contemplative community in one of Rome's suburbs. I met a woman so immersed in the divine mysteries that her face radiated God's love.

CLOWNING IN ROME

SEND IN THE CLOWNS

I met many holy men and women offering their lives to others with a disarming generosity. And slowly, I started to realize that in the great circus of Rome, full of lion-tamers and trapeze artists whose dazzling feats claim our attention, the real and true story was told by the clowns.

Clowns are not in the centre of the events. They appear between the great acts, fumble and fall, and make us smile again after the tensions created by the heroes we came to admire. The clowns don't have it together, they do not succeed in what they try, they are awkward, out of balance, and left-handed, but . . . they are on our side. We respond to them not with admiration but with sympathy, not with amazement but with understanding, not with tension but with a smile. Of the virtuosi we say, "How do they do it?" Of the clowns we say, "They are like us." The clowns remind us with a tear and a smile that we share the same human weaknesses. . . .

The longer I was in Rome, the more I enjoyed the clowns, those peripheral people who by their humble, saintly lives evoke a smile and awaken hope, even in a city terrorized by kidnapping and street violence. It is false to think that the Church in Rome is nothing more than an unimaginative bureaucracy, nothing less than a rigid bulwark of conservatism, or nothing other than a splendid museum of renaissance art. There are too many clowns in Rome, both inside and outside the Vatican, who contradict such ideas. I even came to feel that behind the black, purple, and red in the Roman churches, and behind the suits and ties in the Roman offices, there is enough clownishness left not to give up hope.

CLOWNING IN ROME

A DIVINE PLACE

When I met Mother Teresa in Rome, I saw immediately that her inner attention was focused constantly on Jesus. It seemed that she saw only him and through him came to see the poorest of the poor to whom she has dedicated her life. She never answers the many psychological and socio-economic questions brought to her on the level they are raised. She answers them with a logic, from a perspective, and in a place that remains unfamiliar to most of us. It is a divine logic, a divine perspective, a divine place. That is why many find her simplistic, naïve, and out of touch with the "real problems." Like

Jesus himself, she challenges her listeners to move with her to that place from where things can be seen as God sees them.

When I explained to her all my problems and struggles with elaborate details and asked for her insights, she simply said: "If you spend one hour a day in contemplative prayer and never do anything which you know is wrong, you will be all right." With these words she answered none as well as all of my problems at the same time. It was now up to me to be willing to move to the place where that answer could be heard.

¡GRACIAS!

A CHURCH IN PICCADILLY

I am spending a few days in London. This afternoon I visited Donald Reeves, the pastor of St. James's Anglican church in Piccadilly.

Donald Reeves is a man of many gifts: He is an activist, a contemplative, a social worker, an artist, a caring pastor, a restless mover, a visionary, and a pragmatist. In five years he converted a practically lifeless downtown Anglican parish into a vibrant centre of prayer and action. When I arrived at the rectory I could sense the vibrancy of the place: Within minutes I had met a bishop, a Jew, an ex-convict, an artist, and an administrator. Donald introduced them all to me with words of praise and encouragement. You could sense that people were doing new things here, things they believed in. The parish is a place for meditation, counseling, art events, concerts, peacemaking, book publishing, and hospitality. It is a place that welcomes traditional Christians as well as people who feel alienated from the Church. It is an incredibly diverse place, embracing charismatics as well as activists, Christians as well as non-Christians.

Listening to Donald, I realized how much he had been influenced by new communities in the United States, especially the Sojourners' Fellowship and the Church of the Savior in Washington D.C. I felt invigorated just being with him and walking around the place with him. I was ready to promise all sorts of things: lectures, retreats, writing, conversations, and discussions. But I controlled my impulse to help and asked for simple fellowship instead. Being connected with this church as a friend, a supporter, and a fellow traveler seems most important of all.

THE ROAD TO DAYBREAK

A STUDIO IN SOHO

I spent the whole day with Bart Gavigan and Patricia Beall. They first came to see me in Cambridge in May 1985, while they were preparing a film about George Zabelka, the Air Force chaplain turned pacifist. Although we had met for only a few hours, we had experienced a deep bond among us and a sense that Jesus had brought us together to support each other in our spiritual journeys. . . .

After celebrating the Eucharist together in the parish church and having a meal in a London restaurant, we went to the Soho district, where Bart had rented a studio to cut *The Reluctant Prophet*, the film about George Zabelka that is now in its final stage of editing. It was quite an experience for me. We walked through the crowded district full of market stalls, porno shops, and shouting people. In the middle of all this craziness, we found Bart's little cutting room. Then we sat watching the beginning of a gripping documentary about the priest who, after having blessed those who dropped the atomic bomb on Hiroshima, was converted to a committed peacemaker. It struck me that we were sitting in a dark upstairs studio watching a film about peacemaking while voices of lust and violence surrounded us on all sides.

Bart is a very unusual filmmaker. When he discovered that in most filmmaking the communication of ideas and ideals is completely subservient to the making of profits, he joined a Christian community to test his priorities. Now, many years later, he is ready to make films, not for money, but to follow Jesus' way. In this lustful and violent world he has to risk his money and reputation to do what he feels called to do, but he is determined to do what is just and right, and he trusts that the rest will be given to him.

THE ROAD TO DAYBREAK

SACRAMENTAL IRELAND

Every time I am in Ireland, I am struck with the different rhythm of life. Because of my jet lag, I decided to "sleep in" until 9:00 a.m. But when I arrived at the breakfast table at 9:30, I was one of the first! No hurry, no urgencies. As they say in Ireland: "God created time, and He created plenty of it."

My visit to Ireland has a long history. In 1961 I presided over the wedding of Sophie and Seamus and in 1966 over the wedding of Leonie and Paddy. Their weddings took place in Holland, but both couples moved to Cork, Ireland, where Seamus is a businessman and Paddy a surgeon.

Last year I came to Ireland to preside over the marriage of David, the oldest child of Sophie and Seamus, to Mary, and now I am here again to celebrate the marriage of Leonietje, the oldest daughter of Leonie and Paddy, to Morgan. . . .

At 3:00 p.m. we arrived at Kenmare, where the wedding will take place. When evening came, all the wedding guests gathered for a barbecue. I was amazed by the people from many parts of the world who had traveled here for this wedding. There was a group of friends from New Zealand and a large group of family from Holland. People had also come from Hong Kong, China, Zimbabwe, South Africa, Denmark, the USA, and England. All together there were about 170 guests, all living together for a weekend.

Talking to so many people from so many parts of the world, I couldn't but marvel at the ways people get connected and grieve for the fact that there still are so many mental, psychological, and religious distances on our small planet. If it is possible to come from the ends of the earth to celebrate the commitment of a man and a woman to each other, why does it remain impossible to stop people from killing each other because of religious, social, and economic differences?

Restless thoughts in the most restful surroundings....

Even though I have been the celebrant at many weddings, every time again I feel quite nervous and anxious. There seem to be so many details that I am seldom very peaceful inside until it is over.

The celebration took place at 2:00 p.m. It was a very beautiful and festive liturgy. The Gospel from John about the great commandment to love one another prompted my words about care: care for your own heart, care for each other, and care for others.

At communion time I asked everyone to come to the front to receive the consecrated bread or a word of blessing and encouragement. Many came for a blessing, and quite a few of those who had come to receive the host came up to me later and asked for a blessing. So I have been speaking words of blessing to many people during the afternoon. I realize how deeply people are touched by simple words of reassurance, encouragement, and empowerment spoken in the Name of God.

SABBATICAL JOURNEY

... In Cork, David and Mary were waiting for me to baptize Cian, their four-month-old boy. Before the baptism I spoke a little with David and Mary about the significance of baptism. I tried to explain that it is a proclamation that the child is not the property of the parents but a gift of God to be welcomed into the human community and led to the freedom of the children of God. Mary said, "It is often hard to realize that I do not own my little Cian, but as I see him growing so fast I realize that he has been leaving me from the moment he was born. Yes, I feel a certain sadness when I see him growing up so soon." A little later a small circle of family gathered around Cian. He was crying, so we needed time to let him fall asleep and receive all the baptismal blessings. The oils, the water, the white cloth, and the burning candle became real signs of transformation and hope in this small circle of family and friends. David commented that it was "unbelievably special." In such a simple context, baptism is not a ritual or a ceremony but an event that directly touches and affects our lives.

SABBATICAL JOURNEY

NORTH AMERICA

Toronto, Ontario, Canada

Winnipeg, Manitoba, Canada

New York, New York

Washington, D.C.

Santa Fe, New Mexico

Chimayó, New Mexico

San Francisco, California

San Diego, California

Cancún, Mexico

THE ONTARIO WATERLINE

From the bay windows of Hans and Margaret's house I have a splendid view of Lake Ontario. My eyes are continually drawn to the mysterious line where water and sky touch each other. It is blue touching gray, or gray touching blue, or blue touching blue, or gray touching gray. Endless shades of blue and endless shades of gray. It is like an abstract painting in which everything is reduced to one line, but a line that connects heaven and earth, soul and body, life and death.

Just focusing on that line is meditating. It quiets my heart and mind and brings me a sense of belonging that transcends the limitations of my daily existence. Most often the water and sky are empty, but once in a while a sailboat or a plane passes by in the distance, neither of them ever crossing the line. Crossing the line means death.

Last Sunday during the Canadian National Exhibition Air Show, a Royal Air Force Nimrod with seven airmen onboard plunged into Lake Ontario. None of the crew survived. The blue sky became a treacherous vault, and the peaceful, glistening water a devouring monster. And that line became a tightrope from which you cannot fall without losing everything.

I must keep looking at that line. It forces me to face life and death, goodness and evil, gentleness and force, and cracks open my heart to experience the depth of being.

Now the darkness gradually covers it all. The line vanishes from sight, and everything falls silent.

SABBATICAL JOURNEY

THE TORONTO SKYLINE

Since I have been with Hans and Margaret, I have driven several times to downtown Toronto. The ride on the QEW (Queen Elizabeth Way) and the Gardiner Expressway gives me an experience of the city no other highway gives. On the QEW, I see the CN Tower with the Sky-Dome and its surrounding high-rise buildings gradually appearing before my eyes. Then when the QEW ends and I drive up on the elevated Gardiner Expressway, all these tall buildings become like a huge theatre set where a great show is going to be performed.

For the first time I have the feeling that I love Toronto! I do not think I have ever loved a city. I lived in South Bend, Indiana, in New Haven, Connecticut, and in Cambridge, Massachusetts, but I have never felt any attachment to these places. Nor do I feel much affinity to the several Dutch towns and cities where I have lived before coming to North America. But after nine years in Toronto, I am starting to feel that this is my city, and that I belong here.

I was deeply moved when, arriving by ship from Holland, I first saw the New York skyline. I was overwhelmed by the view of the Chicago skyline when a friend drove me for the first time on Lake Shore Drive. And the skylines of San Francisco, Dallas, and Houston have imprinted themselves on my mind as pictures I will never forget. But when I saw the Toronto skyline several times this week, I heard myself saying, "This is my city, this is my home, and I am excited about it. It is beautiful. I am proud to live here." It is a wonderful sensation. It is the sensation of belonging.

Last night I invited two Daybreak friends, Carrie and Geoff, for dinner at the revolving restaurant on the top of the CN Tower. From the large restaurant windows we saw the city turning beneath us. Within seventy minutes we saw the Toronto Islands, the Harbourfront, Ontario Place, the Music Hall, City Hall, the Convention Centre, the Royal York Hotel, and the railroad station, with its many tracks going west and east. We saw planes coming and going, boats moving on the lake, and thousands of cars crawling on the expressway. Overseeing the city in this way I felt the desire to come to know it better and to make it truly *my* city, a city I can love.

SABBATICAL JOURNEY

REFLECTING IN WINNIPEG

You have an idea of what the new country looks like. Still, you are very much at home, although not truly at peace, in the old country. You know the ways of the old country, its joys and pains, its happy and sad moments. You have spent most of your days there. Even though you know that you have not found there what your heart most desires, you remain quite attached to it. It has become part of your very bones.

Now you have come to realize that you must leave it and enter the new country, where your Beloved dwells. You know that what helped and guided you in the old country no longer works, but what else do you have to go by? You are being asked to trust that you will find what you need in the new country. That requires the death of what has become so precious to you: influence, success, yes, even affection and praise.

Trust is so hard, since you have nothing to fall back on. Still, trust is what is essential. The new country is where you are called to go, and the only way to go there is naked and vulnerable.

It seems that you keep crossing and recrossing the border. For a while you experience a real joy in the new country. But then you feel afraid and start longing again for all you left behind, so you go back to the old country. To your dismay, you discover that the old country has lost its charm. Risk a few more steps into the new country, trusting that each time you enter it, you will feel more comfortable and be able to stay longer.

THE INNER VOICE OF LOVE

MANHATTAN TRANSFER

It is 6:00 p.m., and I am sitting behind the little antique desk in the guest room of my friends Wendy and Jay in Manhattan.

I vividly remember when I arrived for the first time in New York. I came from Holland on the

Maardam, one of the passenger ships of the Holland–America line. It was a "free" trip because I had been given the position of Catholic chaplain for the Dutch emigrants. It was in the early sixties. I can still recall the feeling I had when at 7:00 in the morning we passed the Statue of Liberty and approached the imposing skyline of Manhattan Island. With me, looking at the view, was Zita, the exiled empress of Austria, one of the many passengers I had met during the trip. I took her picture with the skyscrapers in the background. I was all excited about New York, about Zita, and about coming to the New World for the first time.

Now, thirty-four years later, I have come to know New York, its beauty and its ugliness, its wealth and its poverty, its open parks and little alleys, its splendor and its squalor. But I am no longer a tourist here. For many years New York remained for me a place with incredible sights to see: the Empire State Building, the United Nations buildings, Rockefeller Center, St. Patrick's Cathedral, the Metropolitan Museum, Times Square, Broadway, Fifth Avenue. . . . I saw them all and took photographs of them all.

But then I came to know New Yorkers, people who had lived in New York all their lives, worked there, went to church there, and had their circles of friends there. Gradually New York City became smaller, friendlier, more intimate, and much safer for me.

Tonight I am just full of gratitude for being invited into this city by good friends, Wendy and Jay, and by other loving and generous people. Through them and many others, the United States has become my country. And although I now have my home in Canada, I still feel very much at home in this country and especially in this city.

SABBATICAL JOURNEY

MAHLER AT CARNEGIE HALL

This afternoon at three o'clock Wendy and I went to a Gustav Mahler concert at Carnegie Hall [in New York]. The program consisted of the "Kindertotenlieder" and the Sixth Symphony. The orchestra was the Metropolitan Opera Orchestra, the conductor, James Levine, and the soloist, the bass-baritone Bryn Terfel, a native of North Wales.

Many weeks ago Wendy had invited me to go with her to this unique event. It was an unforgettable experience. Just being at Carnegie Hall for the first time was a real treat.

I had never heard Mahler's "Kindertotenlieder." They are based on poems by the German poet Friedrich Rückert (1788–1866), written as an expression of grief at the death, from scarlet fever, of his children Louise and Ernst in January 1833. Gustav Mahler, who had grieved deeply over the loss of his fourteen-year-old brother, Ernst, set to music five of Rückert's "Songs on the Death of Children. . . ."

After the intermission Levine directed the Sixth Symphony. It is considered one of Mahler's greatest works and expresses a great range of emotion—exuberant joy, intense anguish, pastoral serenity, great pain, sadness, fear, hope, and despair. Everything is intense, elaborate, and majestic. The orchestra was the largest I had ever seen. During the eighty-one minute performance, I mostly looked—with Wendy's binoculars—at the percussion section. There were seven men moving from one instrument to the other, trying to keep up with the various sounds they had to produce. For certain periods, I became so fascinated by their actions and interactions that I forgot to listen to the music. These men in grey suits and ties looked dead serious, in stark contrast to the joyful noises they were making. Especially one man with a strikingly beautiful, deeply carved face and long black hair, handling the large brass cymbals,

[who] went about his business without the slightest change of expression. While looking at these figures I started to wonder what their lives looked like outside of Carnegie Hall or Lincoln Center.

SABBATICAL JOURNEY

THE PLACE OF POVERTY

Murray is a New York banker who personally knows countless people I have only heard about on TV or read about in the newspapers. He has read many of my books and feels that his world needs the word of God as much as my world does. It was a very humbling experience to hear a man who knows "the best and the brightest" say, "Give us a word from God, speak to us about Jesus . . . do not stay away from the rich, who are so poor."

Jesus loves the poor—but poverty takes many forms. How easily I forget that fact, leaving the powerful, the famous, and the successful without the spiritual food they crave. But to offer that food, I have to be very poor myself—not curious, not ambitious, not pretentious, not proud. It is so easy to be swept off one's own feet by the glitter of the world, seduced by its apparent splendor. And yet the only place I can really be is the place of poverty, the place where there is loneliness, anger, confusion, depression, and pain. I have to go there in the name of Jesus, staying close to his name and offering his love.

O Lord, help me not to be distracted by power and wealth; help me not to be impressed by knowing the stars and heroes of this world. Open my eyes to the suffering heart of your people whoever they are, and give me the word that can bring healing and consolation. Amen.

THE ROAD TO DAYBREAK

WASHINGTON D.C. AND THE U.S. SENATE

Having lunch with Senator Mark Hatfield in the stately quarters of the Senate Appropriations Committee, hearing about the struggle against the fabrication of nerve gas and the attempts to get some solid information about human rights violations in Guatemala, meeting Henry Kissinger in the corridor, and sensing the general atmosphere of busyness and urgency—all of this gave me ample occasion to leave the house of the Lord and roam around curiously searching for power, influence, and success.

Yet all day Jesus remained in the centre, and the hours were filled with a sense of God's presence.

What most impressed me was the eagerness of all the people I met today to hear about God's presence in this world. It seemed as if I couldn't say enough about it. During my two-hour luncheon with Senator Hatfield and his aides, not a minute was spent talking about politics. All our attention went to questions about the message of the New Testament, living a fruitful life, developing meaningful relationships, prayer, obedience, and faithfulness. As we were talking, I realized that, in fact, we were coming closer to the real problems of the world than a debate on current political issues would have brought us.

At one point in our conversation, I asked Senator Hatfield, "How can I be of any help to the U.S. Senate?" He said, "Come and speak to us about forgiveness, reconciliation, and ways to live in peace with one another. So much bitterness and resentment, jealousy and anger exist in the lives of politicians, at work as well as at home, that any healing word will be received with open hands." Later, Doug Coe asked me to give a retreat to twenty members of the young presidents' organization. I asked him, "Who are the young presidents?" He said, "They are people, mostly men, who have made more than a million dollars before they were thirty years old, who head a company with at least fifty employees, and who have significant influence." I asked, "Why do they want a retreat?" He answered, "They have a great desire to come to know Jesus. They will come to any place in the world, on any day you want, to hear you speak about Jesus."

How much more do I have to know? Why should I want anything but Jesus, where everyone I meet asks me to proclaim him? My only task is to stay in God's house and stop roaming around in the world.

THE ROAD TO DAYBREAK

AGONY AND ECSTASY IN NEW MEXICO

The days in Santa Fe, simple and unpretentious as they were, revealed to me in a new way the beauty of life. Friendship, art, nature, history, and the tangible presence of the immanent as well as transcendent love of God filled me with gratitude for being alive and being alive with others.

In Santa Fe both agony and ecstasy are imprinted on the buildings and monuments and reflected in the many adobe houses. I well understand why painters, sculptors, writers and musicians like to live there. Many great people have left their spirits in Santa Fe to protect as well as inspire them. During this short stay I experienced the presence of these spirits and got a glimpse of the permanent reality shining through the impermanence of all created things.

SABBATICAL JOURNEY

. . . After lunch I bought a short biography of the painter Georgia O'Keeffe by Michael Berry. The more I read about O'Keeffe and look at her paintings, the more I feel a deep affinity with her. She struggled in relationships, especially in her relationship with the photographer Alfred Stieglitz. Her struggles to develop her own art form—going back and forth between New York and New Mexico—reveal a person with a great need for love, affection, and personal support, but also for independence, freedom, solitude, and space for creativity. She definitely belongs to New Mexico. As I walk around Santa Fe looking at the sky, the buildings, and the flowers, and letting the colors of this milieu affect me, I realize that indeed nature imitates art. O'Keeffe's paintings make me *see* Santa Fe. Just as Rembrandt and several other Dutch painters opened Vincent van Gogh's eyes to really *see* the landscape he was walking through, O'Keeffe gives me eyes to see the world that surrounds me.

Why is Georgia O'Keeffe so popular? I think it is the combination of her personality and her art. Just as Vincent's story and his art cannot be separated, so Georgia's story and her art belong together. It's not just her paintings that hold me in their grip; it's also this most remarkable woman, whose intense search for intimacy and solitude is part of the art she created. Seeing her art is seeing her life, and seeing her life is helping me see my own.

SABBATICAL JOURNEY

HOLY DIRT

We drove for a good half-hour through the desert [of New Mexico] and arrived around noon at the charming looking church of Chimayó, a small adobe structure with two towers and a lovely walled-in courtyard in front of it. The intimate building is often called the Lourdes of America. Every year close to three hundred thousand people come from far and wide, often on foot, to pray for peace in the world and in their hearts, to fulfill a promise, or to seek healing.

The miraculous crucifix found around 1810 forms the centre of the shrine. There also is an adjacent room with a little well, El Pozito, with "holy dirt" that people cross themselves with and take home. Like Lourdes water, the holy dirt of Chimayó helps people in their prayers for healing.

When Wayne, Frank and I entered the little church we were engulfed by an atmosphere of prayer. You could feel that, for more than a century and a half, people had filled the intimate space with their cries, tears, and words of thanks and praise. The crucifix on the main altar, surrounded by a reredos of painted symbols, is deeply moving. The face of Christ is gentle and loving even in his agony. We prayed for a while and went to the El Pozito, where people were kneeling and crossing themselves with the dry sand.

SABBATICAL JOURNEY

THE SENSUALITY OF CALIFORNIA

It must be one of the most beautiful spots in the world. I am looking out over San Francisco Bay. In the far distance I recognize the lighthouse of Alcatraz Island, and behind it the outline of the Golden Gate Bridge. As the darkness slowly covers the bay area, the view is gradually transformed by a myriad of lights telling me of all the different people living around the water. It is very quiet on the balcony [at Berkeley]—the city is not too far away to hear its sounds. The air is gentle and warm, full of scents coming from the blooming trees. . . . I marvel at being alive and being able to be part of it all.

Being in California is exciting as well as disturbing to me. It is very hard for me to describe the emotions this world calls forth in me. The pleasant climate, the lush gardens, the splendid trees and flowerbeds, the beautiful view over the bay, the city, the island, and the bridges call forth in me words of praise, gratitude, and joy. But the countless car lots, the intense traffic, the huge advertisements, the new buildings going up all over the place, the smog, the noises, the fastness of living—all of this makes me feel unconnected, lonely, and a little lost.

Maybe the word that summarizes it all is "sensual." All my senses are being stimulated, but with very little grounding, very little history, very little spirit. I keep wondering how my heart can be fed in this world. It seems as if everyone is moving quickly to meet some person or go to some place or some event. But nobody has much of a home. The houses look very temporary. They will probably last a few decades, maybe a century, but then something else will take their place.

The people we meet are very friendly, easygoing, casual, and entertaining; but I keep wondering how to be with them, how to speak with them, how to pray with them. Everything is very open, expressive and new; but I find myself looking for a space that is hidden, silent, and old. This is a land to which people go in order to be free from tradition, constraints, and an oppressive history. But the price for this freedom is high: individualism, competition, rootlessness, and frequently loneliness and a sense of being lost. When anything goes, everything is allowed, everything is worth a try, then nothing is sacred, nothing venerable, nothing worth much respect. Being young, daring, original, and mobile seems to be the ideal. Old things need to be replaced by new things, and old people are to be pitied.

The body is central. The sun, the beaches, the water, and the lushness of nature open up all the senses. But it is hard to experience the body as the temple of the spirit. That requires a very special discipline. To reach that inner sanctum where God's voice can be heard and obeyed is not easy if you are always called outward. It is not surprising that California has become a place where many spiritual disciplines are being discovered, studied, and practiced. There are many meditation centers—Buddhist, Christian, and nonreligious. More and more people feel a need to discover an inner anchor to keep themselves whole in the midst of the sensual world.

THE ROAD TO DAYBREAK

PAIN AND PRESENCE IN SAN FRANCISCO

I didn't know John very well, but a few years ago when I was in San Francisco, Rose introduced me to him and we spent some time together. John told me about his homosexuality and his life in the San Francisco gay community. He did not try to defend his way of living or apologize for it. I remember his great compassion for the people he spoke about, but also his critical remarks about snobbism [*sic*] and capitalism in the San Francisco gay community. He himself was extremely generous. He gave much of his time, money, and energy to people in need and asked very little for himself. Seldom have I known anyone who was so eager to have me understand and learn. He was so nonjudgmental, self-possessed, and honest that I came to think of him as an example of a just man.

Last February, Rose called me in Cambridge [Massachusetts] to tell me that John was very sick with AIDS. I immediately flew to San Francisco and spent a day with Rose at her home and with John and his friend Mike in the hospital. John asked me to read the Twenty-third Psalm with him. It was the psalm he remembered, the psalm his father had prayed with him. It was a psalm that gave him peace. We prayed the words together several times:

> The Lord is my shepherd,
> there is nothing I shall want.
> Fresh and green are the pastures
> where he gives me repose.
> Near restful waters he leads me
> to revive my drooping spirit.

. . . My time with John and Rose showed me the ravaging power of AIDS. John could hardly stay quiet for a minute. Like a wild animal caught in a cage, he could find no rest, and his whole body moved in pain. To see his agony and not be able to do anything, to know that he would only get worse, was nearly intolerable. But I was struck by the care which surrounded him. Many AIDS patients are rejected by family and friends. But Rose's love for her son grew stronger every day of his illness. No condemnation, no accusation, no rejection, but love as only a mother can give. And Mike, John's companion, gave every minute of his time and every ounce of his energy to his sick friend. No complaints, no irritation, just faithful presence.

THE ROAD TO DAYBREAK

LOVE AND THE CASTRO

As my friend and I walked through the busy streets to find a restaurant, I thought of John. A few years ago he showed me the district and told me all about the life there. Then the word "AIDS" was hardly known. Now John is dead after a long, devastating illness, and many have shared his agony.

Behind a façade of opulent wealth, a great variety of entertainment, large stores with posters, printed T-shirts, greeting cards, and all sorts of playful knickknacks lies an immense fear. And not only fear but also guilt, feelings of rejection, anger, fatalism, careless hedonism, and, in the midst of it all, trust, hope, love, and the rediscovery of God in the face of death.

As I walked with my friend on the streets of the Castro district, we saw countless men walking up and down the sidewalks just looking at each other, gazing into store windows, standing on corners in small groups, and going in and out of bars, theatres, video shops, drugstores, and restaurants. It seemed as if everyone was waiting for something that would bring them a sense of being deeply loved, fully accepted, and truly at home. But evident in the eyes of many was deep suffering, anguish, and loneliness, because what they most seek and most desire seems most elusive. Many have not been able to find a lasting home or a safe relationship, and now, with the AIDS threat, fear has become all-pervasive.

And yet AIDS has unleashed not only fear, but also an enormous generosity. Many people are showing great care for each other, great courage in helping each other, great faithfulness, and often unwavering love. I sensed an enormous need for God's love to be made known to these fearful and often generous people. More than ever the Church has to live out Christ's love for the poor, the sinners, the publicans, the rejected, the possessed, and all who desperately need to be loved. As I saw the countless gay men on the streets, I kept thinking about the great consolation that Jesus came to offer. He revealed the total and unlimited love of God for humanity. This is the love that the Church is called to make visible, not by judging, condemning, or segregating, but by serving everyone in need. I often wonder if the many heated debates about the morality of homosexuality do not prevent the Christian community from reaching out fearlessly to its suffering fellow humans.

THE ROAD TO DAYBREAK

CHRISTMAS IN SAN DIEGO

This morning Jonas drove me to the airport. It was snowing, and I was nervous because Sue's plane was a half hour late. When she arrived, shortly before 10:00 a.m., Jonas said hello and good-bye to Sue, our plane was deiced and, just before the snowstorm clouded over the airport, we were on our way.

At the San Diego Airport we were met, and forty minutes later we arrived at Joan's estate. It was a wonderful beginning because Joan's welcome was so warm and she wanted us to feel right at home. While showing us to our rooms, she took us through her gorgeous, elegant home. Wherever we walked, we saw the most precious artifacts, vases with fresh flowers, and elegant tapestries. There was much activity around the swimming pool on the patio, where a large tent had been set up. A crew of men were at work making everything ready for tomorrow night's Christmas party. As it became dark the whole garden lit up with what seemed myriads of little lights. In the trees, large shining stars were hung, and the entrance road and the hedges surrounding the estate were all decorated with countless white and red Christmas lights.

. . . After an elegant breakfast we all drove to the San Diego Hospice, where Sue and I had been asked to speak about "a spirituality of care." About a hundred people were gathered.

For many years Joan had dreamed about a freestanding hospice in San Diego. After a complex struggle to get the necessary permissions, the wonderful building with twenty-four rooms was constructed on a cliff overlooking the city. The staff is very gentle and friendly, and the atmosphere is homey and quite intimate. Both Sue and I spoke about preparing ourselves and others for "dying well." We sang some Taizé songs and had a lively exchange with the audience. We also met with the pastoral ministers of the hospice. It was a very good morning, and we all felt quite uplifted.

At 6.00 p.m. Joan's Christmas party began. About ninety people arrived. A small choir sang some Christmas carols, and a large group of servers offered a great variety of drinks and snacks. The surroundings were spectacular, the food delicious, the conversations friendly, the music pleasant, and everything very, very elegant. Joan is a perfect hostess, and she moved among her many guests with ease. She has a gift for making people feel special. Everyone enjoyed the warm and friendly atmosphere. By 10:00 p.m. most of the guests had left. I went to bed somewhat dazzled, puzzled, and intrigued by the life I had been part of today. . . .

At 8:30 a.m. Phil drove us to downtown San Diego to visit the homeless shelter founded and led by Father Joe. I had met him at the Christmas party and expressed to him my desire to see his place. . . . He showed us the building for permanent residents, the buildings for women and men who can stay only at night but are on the streets during the day, a new medical centre with dental and eye clinics, and the daily food centre. As we walked across the patio, a long line of women and men were waiting for their meal. Many volunteers from Christian, Buddhist, and Mormon groups were busy preparing and serving the meals, clearing the tables, and doing the dishes. Father Joe has a vision about the way the homeless can gradually be motivated to move from coming to the food line, to spending nights at the shelter, to becoming permanent residents, to getting job training, to finding employment, to reclaiming their full human dignity. . . . When we returned to Joan's estate, we celebrated the Eucharist together in the garden in front of the Mexican crèche. It was a very peaceful liturgy. We sat around the little table, read the readings, shared our reflections, prayed, and received the sacred gifts of the Body and Blood of Christ.

Joan's granddaughter and her boyfriend then joined our little party, and we drove to the harbor, where we saw from a distance Joan's magnificent yacht decorated with Christmas lights. The seven-man crew were standing on the dock to greet us. As soon as we were onboard, we started our harbor cruise. Phil gave us a tour of the boat. We admired the spacious lounge with separate dining space, beautiful bedrooms, a very well-equipped kitchen, the exercise room, and the large sundeck. On the bridge the captain and his crew explained some of the high-tech navigational equipment.

After the tour we were invited to a splendidly decorated table for dinner. As we ate, we slowly "sailed" past the impressive San Diego skyline, went under the high Coronado Bridge, and had a view of the navy aircraft carriers. Christmas lights were all over, decorating the skyscrapers, the big hotels, and the ships in the harbor. . . .

Sue's famous question "What *does* it all mean?" is mine after this moving trip, on which I experienced, met, and spoke with wonderful people who came from a world of abundance, and with beautiful people who were radically poor, close to death, and in dire need. I ponder my experience, and I recognize once more that the way for us to be in this world is to focus on the spiritual life—our own as well as the spiritual life of each one of the people that we meet.

SABBATICAL JOURNEY

ABUNDANCE IN MEXICO

I am on my way to Cancún, Mexico. At 6:30 this morning, I left from Logan Airport in Boston to fly to Dallas. . . . What's going on in Cancún? A three-day meeting of The Gathering, an evangelical support network for philanthropists, who come together once a year to support and encourage one another in their philanthropic work and to discuss how to give in the spirit of the Gospel. In order to be "eligible" for The Gathering, each member must be a major donor to a charitable organization. . . .

Jesus' words "You cannot serve God and wealth" are the guideline of those who will meet in Cancún. . . . Most important for me is that I can speak as a member of a community where the poor form the centre.

. . . Here we are at the very luxurious Ritz-Carlton Hotel, with three restaurants, two large outdoor swimming pools, a large reception area, huge ballrooms, wide, curving staircases, great glittering chandeliers, and many little shops with very expensive items. All of it looks out on the blue, sun-washed Caribbean Sea.

The Mexican personnel are extremely friendly. They all are English-speaking young men and women, obviously very well trained in their jobs. Their most used expression is "my pleasure." They say it so often and with such a sympathetic Mexican accent that it starts sounding like a sacred mantra.

. . . My morning reflections on the story of the multiplication of bread seemed to be well received. I spoke about compassion, scarcity, gifts, abundance and solitude, following the different moments in the story, and I tried to show what it means to also give ourselves to others. The main idea was that our gifts, small as they may seem, become great by being recognized as God's gifts for God's people. When we refrain from giving, with a scarcity mentality, the little we have will become less. When we give generously, with an abundance mentality, what we give away will multiply.

SABBATICAL JOURNEY

HIGHS AND LOWS

Our last day in Cancún. . . . we celebrated the Eucharist together and had lunch on the terrace of the hotel. Nathan suggested I ride in one of the parachutes that are pulled by little motorboats, taking you high above the hotels and giving you a grand view of the Cancún area. I said that I would go if we could go together. Three Mexican boys running the offshore operation strapped us in our "seats," put on our swimming vests, made us bend our knees while holding tight to our straps, and waved to the motorboat to pull us up. A few seconds later we were hanging in the sky! Nice breeze, nice view, nice sensation. The boat pulled us above the beach and the water for about fifteen minutes. As we returned we missed our landing spot, and we saw the boys waving and telling us to pull our red flag to steer the parachute to the beach. But we didn't make it and ended up in the rolling waves. The boys ran out to disentangle us from all the ropes, vests, and straps and lead us back to the beach.

SABBATICAL JOURNEY

UNIVERSALITY

Many of the people I met in Cancún believe that without an explicit personal profession of faith in Jesus as our Lord and Savior, we cannot make it to heaven. They are convinced that God has called us to convert every human being to Jesus.

This vision inspires much generosity, commitment, and a great worldwide project. Not a few of the men and women we met had traveled far and wide, put their lives and health in danger, given large parts of their personal income, and taken many financial risks. Their love for Jesus is deep, intense, and radical. They spoke about Jesus fearlessly and were prepared for rejection and ridicule. They are very committed disciples, not hesitant to pay the cost of discipleship.

Still . . . I felt somewhat uncomfortable, even though this belief was present in my own upbringing. My conviction as a young man was that there is no salvation outside the Catholic Church and that it was my task to bring all "non-believers" into the one true church.

But much has happened to me over the years. My own psychological training, my exposure to people from the most different religious backgrounds, the Second Vatican Council, the new theology of mission, and my life at L'Arche have all deepened and broadened my views on Jesus' saving work. Today I personally believe that, while Jesus came to open the door to God's house, all human beings can walk through that door, whether they know about Jesus or not. Today I see it as my call to help every person claim his or her own way to God. I feel deeply called to witness for Jesus as the one who is the source of my own spiritual journey and thus create the possibility for other people to know Jesus and commit themselves to him. I am so truly convinced that the Spirit of God is present in our midst and that each person can be touched by God's Spirit in ways far beyond my own comprehension and intention.

SABBATICAL JOURNEY

CENTRAL AND LATIN AMERICA

Jalapa, Nicaragua

Lima, Peru

Pamplona Alta, Peru

Cochabamba, Peru

Cuzco, Peru

THE WOMEN OF NICARAGUA

I would never have been able to say this with such confidence if I had not witnessed the presence of the risen Lord among the suffering people of Nicaragua. It was in fact a very concrete event on the border between Nicaragua and Honduras that made it possible for me to say: "Christ is risen, He is risen indeed." I even dare to say that what I saw and heard there was the most revealing experience of my visit to Central America. . . . With 150 North Americans I went to Jalapa, a small Nicaraguan town very close to the Honduran border. Jalapa had been the victim of many attacks by the counter-revolutionaries who have their camps in the southern part of Honduras and regularly enter into Nicaragua with the purpose of establishing a bridgehead there and gradually undermining the Sandinista regime. During the month prior to our visit, many people in the Jalapa area had suffered severely from these hostilities. This was the reason we wanted to go there. We wanted to have some first-hand experience of war going on between Honduras and Nicaragua, and pray for peace with the people who had suffered from that war.

I vividly remember how, during the prayer vigil, five Nicaraguan women joined us. They stood very close to each other and quietly spoke to a group of about 20 North Americans. It was an intimate gathering of the people huddling together and trying to understand each other. One of the women raised her voice and said, "A few months ago the counter-revolutionaries kidnapped my seventeen-year-old son and took him to Honduras. I have never heard from him anymore and I lie awake during the night wondering if I will ever see him again."

Then another woman spoke: "I had two boys and they both have been killed during the last year. When I grieve and mourn, I grieve and mourn, not only because they have been killed, but also because those who killed them dismembered their bodies and threw the parts over the fields so that I could not even give them a decent burial." Then the third woman spoke: "I had just been married and my husband was working in the fields. Suddenly the contras appeared—they burned the harvest, killed my husband and took his body away. I have never found his body."

There was a long and painful silence. Out of that silence, a voice was heard. One of the Nicaraguan women said, "Do you know that we found US-made weapons in our fields? Do you realize that your government paid for the violence that is taking place here? Are you aware that our children and husbands are being killed because your people make it possible by their support?" Directly or indirectly, willingly or unwillingly, you are causing our agony. Why? Why? What have we done to deserve this? What did we do to you, your people or your country to be subjected to so much hostility, anger, and revenge?"

"Christ of the Americas"

FORGIVENESS AND RESURRECTION AT JALAPA

For a long time no one said a word. What could be said? But then a question came from us that sounded like a prayer. Someone quietly asked, "Do you think you can forgive us? Do you think it is possible for you to speak a word of forgiveness?" I saw how one of the women turned to the others and softly said, "We should forgive them." She then turned to us, looking us in the eye, and said clearly: "Yes, we forgive you." But it seemed that we could not yet fully hear it.

Someone else said, "Do you really forgive us for all the sorrow and pain we have brought to your village and your people?" And the woman said, "Yes, we forgive you." Another voice spoke: "Do you truly forgive us for killing your husbands and children?" And the women said, "Yes, we forgive you." And there was a voice, "Do you also forgive us for all the fear and agony we have brought to your homes?" And the women said, "Yes, we forgive you." And as if we were still not hearing it fully, another begging question was heard, "But do you forgive us too for the many times we have invaded your country in the past and for the fact that we have made you subject to our decisions and rules for most of this century?" And again the women said, "Yes, we forgive you."

Suddenly I realized that I was being lifted up in this litany of forgiveness: "Do you forgive us? Yes, we forgive you. Do you forgive us? Yes, we forgive you." As this prayer was going on, it was as if I could see for a moment that the broken heart of the dying Christ, stretched out on the cross of the Americas, was being healed. The five women appeared as representatives of all men, women and children of Latin and Central America. Their voices were like the voices of millions of people who had suffered during the last five centuries, bringing all the agonies of poverty and oppression together and lifting them up to us. They opened our eyes to the immense suffering that is being suffered by the poor of our countries and said, "Do not be afraid to look at it. We show it to you, not to make you feel guilty or ashamed, but to let you see the immensity of God's forgiveness." The five women of Jalapa are the women standing under the cross. They speak for us that divine prayer: "Father, forgive them, they do not know what they are doing" (Luke 23:34). They are the voices of the dying Christ speaking of new life being born in suffering.

No hatred, no revenge, no lashing out in anger, but repeated words of forgiveness, words that create unity and community. As these words were spoken, the women of Nicaragua and the men and women of North America became one people. They embraced one another, cried together and said over and over again, "Peace, peace, peace be with you." As that was taking place, I and many of us had a glimpse of the resurrection. The risen Christ, the Christ who came to take our sins away by his death, rose to make us into a new body, a new community, a new fellowship, a church. When the North Americans and Nicaraguans became one, they revealed that the power of divine love is stronger than death and reaches far beyond ethnic, national or cultural boundaries.

The forgiveness of the women of Jalapa, offered to us as the fruit of their suffering, gave us a vision of the unity that God's Word came to bring us.

CHRIST OF THE AMERICAS

FLYING INTO LIMA

On the airplane to Lima, I spoke with the woman next to me. She told me that she was returning home with her mother, who had undergone three operations in the United States. "Is your mother better now?" I asked. "Oh yes, she is totally cured," she said with fervent conviction," and the whole family is waiting at the airport to welcome her home." After a few minutes of silence, she wanted to know my reasons for going to Peru. When I told her I was a priest planning to work with the Maryknoll missionaries, her face changed dramatically. She leaned over to me, grabbed my hand, and whispered in an agonized way: "Oh Father, mother has cancer and there is little hope for her."

The first thing I learned about Peruvians was that they have an unlimited trust in priests. Even though the Church certainly has not earned such unconditional respect during the last centuries, the people of Peru give their confidence to their priests without hesitation. This impression was strongly affirmed on Sunday morning, when I found myself in the huge crowd on the Plaza de Armas, welcoming the procession of *el Senor de los milagros* (the Lord of the Miracles). As soon as the bystanders realized that I was a priest, they let go of their inhibitions, handed me their children to lift above the crowds, and told me about their joys and sorrows.

Peru: from the moment I entered it, I felt a deep love for this country. I do not know why. I did not feel this when I went to Chile or Bolivia in the past. But looking at the busy streets of Lima, the dark open faces and the lively gestures, I felt embraced by a loving people in a way I had not known before. Walking through the busy streets, looking at the men, women, and children in their penitential dress—purple habits with white chords—and sensing the gentle spirit of forgiveness, I had the strange emotion of homecoming.

¡Gracias!

THE CITY OF GOD

I was struck not only by the obvious poverty of the people, but also by their dignity. They care for what they own, and they manage to keep little gardens in the midst of this dry, sandy, and dusty place. Thousands of people live here—125,000—but there is space between houses as well as between people. The area is poor, very poor, but not depressing. It is full of visible problems, but not without hope.

Later in the day an elderly laywoman dressed as a nun—Maria is her name—told me about the beginning of the Ciudad de Dios. Ciudad de Dios was the result of a popular invasion on Christmas Eve 1954. Maria remembered that day with a sense of pride. She belonged to the founding fathers and mothers. On that Christmas night, thousands of people illegally occupied the barren land and immediately started to develop it. The government had no choice but to comply and eventually help, and now there is the City of God with countless brick houses, a large church, a school, and several medical posts. The invasion of Ciudad de Dios was one of the first in a long series of similar invasions. Poverty and lack of land forced a constant migration from the countryside to the city. The Indian migrants first lived with relatives and friends; but when they became too numerous and desperate for a space and a livelihood, they organized themselves and seized the barren desert surrounding the city. Today Lima has a large belt of "young towns," many of which are the result of these illegal land seizures.

Pamplona Alta, which belongs to the same parish, developed a few years after Ciudad de Dios was founded. From the many little shacks visible on the bare hills beyond Pamplona Alta, it is clear that invasions—although on a much smaller scale—are still taking place today. . . .

During the evening, I picked up some of Gustavo Gutiérrez's early writings. My visit to Ciudad de Dios makes his words sound very real. This, indeed, is a theology born of solidarity with the people. The people speak about God and his Presence in ways I must slowly come to understand.

¡GRACIAS!

A MEAL WITH THE DEAD

Today I flew from Lima to La Paz and from La Paz to Cochabamba. It was a magnificent flight over Lake Titicaca and over the wild and desolate mountain ranges of Bolivia. . . .

Most of the inhabitants of Cochabamba are Quechua Indians, and their Christianity is pervaded with the religious convictions and practices of the Quechua culture. Although Our Fathers and Hail Marys are constantly recited, it seemed that they only partially express the power of Indian spirituality.

I felt very much part of a mystery that cannot simply be observed and understood, and I started to sympathize even more with the sisters and priests who, after many years in Bolivia, say: "We still can only partially grasp the depth of the Quechua soul." One image stayed uppermost in my mind. It was the image of the boys receiving food for their prayers. The food put on the graves to be eaten with the dead [on All Souls' Day] was given to those who prayed for them. In front of my eyes I saw how prayers became food and food became prayers. I saw how little boys who had to struggle to survive received life from the dead, and how the dead received hope from the little children who prayed for the salvation of their souls. I saw a profound communion between the living and the dead, an intimacy expressed in words and gestures whose significance easily escapes our practical and often skeptical minds.

¡GRACIAS!

FOREIGN TERRAIN

Going to a different culture, in which I find myself again like a child, can become a true psychotherapeutic opportunity. Not everyone is in the position or has the support to use such an opportunity. I have seen much self-righteous, condescending, and even offensive behavior by foreigners towards the people in their host country. Remarks about the laziness, stupidity, and disorganization of Peruvians or Bolivians usually say a lot more about the one who makes such remarks than about Peruvians or Bolivians. Most of the labels by which we pigeonhole people are ways to cope with our own anxiety and insecurity. Many people who suddenly find themselves in a totally unfamiliar milieu decide quickly to label that which is strange to them instead of confronting their own fears and vulnerabilities.

But we can also use the new opportunity for our own healing. When we walk around in a strange milieu, speaking the language haltingly, and feeling out of control and like fools, we can come in touch with a part of ourselves that usually remains hidden behind the thick walls of our defenses. We can come to experience our basic vulnerability, our need for others, our deep-seated feelings of ignorance and inadequacy, and our fundamental dependency. Instead of running away from these scary feelings, we can live through them together and learn that our true value as human beings has its seat far beyond our competence and accomplishments.

¡GRACIAS!

CULTURE SHOCK

One of the most rewarding aspects of living in a strange land is the experience of being loved, not for what we can do, but for who we are. When we become aware that our stuttering, failing vulnerable selves are loved even when we hardly progress, we can let go of our compulsion to prove ourselves and be free to live with others in a fellowship of the weak. That is true healing.

This psychological perspective on culture shock can open up for us a new understanding of God's grace and our vocation to live graceful lives. In the presence of God, we are totally naked, broken, sinful, and dependent, and we realize that we can do nothing, absolutely nothing, without him. When we are willing to confess our true condition, God will embrace us with his love, a love so deep, intimate, and strong that it enables us to make all things new. I am convinced that, for Christians, culture shock can be an opportunity, not only for psychological healing, but also for conversion.

¡GRACIAS!

THE SUFFERING CHRIST

Latin America offers us the image of the suffering Christ. The poor we see every day, the stories about deportation, torture, and murder we hear every day, and the undernourished children we touch every day, reveal to us the suffering Christ hidden within us. When we allow this image of the suffering Christ within us to grow into its full maturity, then ministry to the poor and oppressed becomes a real possibility; because then we can indeed hear, see, and touch him within us as well as among us. Thus prayer becomes ministry and ministry becomes prayer. Once we have seen the suffering Christ within us, we will see him wherever we see people in pain. Once we have seen the suffering Christ among us, we will recognize him in our innermost self.

¡GRACIAS!

THE POWER OF TOUCH

In the Indian culture, no couple will marry in the church without having lived together for some time and without being sure that the woman will be able to bear children. The church ceremony is more an affirmation by the community of their relationship than a beginning of a new life together. When the church becomes involved, the couple has already proven to each other, their friends, and their community that there is a real basis to their union.

What struck me most before, during, and after the event was the lack of any expression of affection whatsoever between the grooms and the brides. They hardly talked to each other; they did not touch each other except when the ritual demanded it. Not one kiss was ever exchanged. Pascual had to remind them repeatedly during the exchange of vows to look at each other, and even that seemed hard for them. When I asked Ann about this later, she said:

"Even in their homes, husband and wife seldom show affection to each other, but both are expressive in their love for their children: they play with them, hug them, kiss them, and touch them constantly."

¡Gracias!

I spent the afternoon with the children of the Catholic orphanage called Gotas de Leche (Drops of Milk). The children were so starved [of] affection that they fought with each other for the privilege of touching me. How little do we really know [about] the power of physical touch. These boys and girls only wanted one thing: to be touched, hugged, stroked, and caressed. Probably most adults have the same needs but no longer have the innocence and unselfconsciousness to express them. Sometimes I see humanity as a sea of people starving for affection, tenderness, care, love, acceptance, forgiveness, and gentleness. Everyone seems to cry: "Please love me." The cry becomes louder and the response so inaudible that people kill each other and themselves in despair. The little orphans tell more than they know. If we don't love one another, we will kill one another. There's no middle road.

¡Gracias!

GOD AND THE DEMON

In times of testing, God and the demon seem close together. Today I felt it more strongly than on other days. . . . As I biked through town and saw groups of young men loitering around the street corners and waiting for the next movie to start; as I walked through the bookstores stacked with magazines about violence, sex, and gossip; and as I saw the endless advertisements for unnecessary items imported mostly from Germany and the United States, I had the feeling of being surrounded by powers much greater than myself. I felt the seductive powers of sin all around me and got a glimpse of the truth that all the horrendous evils which plague our world—hunger, the nuclear arms race, torture, exploitation, rape, child abuse, and all forms of oppression—have their small and sometimes unnoticed beginnings in the human heart. The demon is very patient in the way he goes about his destructive work. I felt the darkness of the world all around me.

After some aimless wandering, I biked to the small Carmelite convent on Avenida America, close to the house of my hosts. A friendly Carmelite sister spoke to me in the chapel and told me that I would be welcome at any hour to come there to pray or celebrate the Eucharist. She radiated a spirit of joy and peace. She told me about the light that shines into the darkness without saying a word about it. As I looked around, I saw the statues of St. Teresa of Avila and St. Thérèse of Lisieux. Suddenly it seemed to me that these two women were talking to me as they had never before. They spoke of another world. As I knelt down in the small and simple chapel, I knew that this place was filled with God's presence. I felt the prayers that had been said there day and night. . . .

My visit to the Carmelite sisters helped me realize again that, where the demon is, God is not far away; and where God shows his presence, the demon does not remain absent very long. There is always a choice to be made between the power of life and the power of death.

¡GRACIAS!

DISPLACEMENT

Tonight Sister Maria Rieckelman spoke about the problems of acculturation. She gave a fine presentation about the many psychological struggles we can experience when we try to find a home in a new culture.

She mentioned Erich Fromm's remark that our two main fears are of losing control and of becoming isolated. I keep experiencing these fears every time I make a move, major or minor, and I wonder if I am getting any better in dealing with them. I find myself with the same old struggles every time I am in a new and unfamiliar milieu. In particular, the experience of isolation keeps returning, not in a lessening but in an increasing degree. Becoming older makes the experience of isolation much more familiar—maybe simply because of sheer repetition—but not less painful.

So, maybe the question is not how to cope better, but how slowly to allow my unchanging character to become a way of humility and surrender to God. As I recognize my fears of being left alone and my desire for a sense of belonging, I may gradually give up my attempts to fill my loneliness and be ready to recognize with my heart that God is Emmanuel, "God-is-with-us," and that I belong to him before anything or anyone else.

¡GRACIAS!

PERUVIAN POUSTINIA

Tonight I finally moved to Pamplona Alta. . . . Pete Ruggere drove me in his blue Volkswagen to my new living quarters with the Oscco-Moreno family. They are his neighbors, and with their help he has built a pleasant room on top of the roof of their house. The word "roof " is a euphemism since this house, like many of the houses in the area, is only half-finished. Construction continues at a variable rate depending on money, need, and time. My little room, therefore, might better be seen as the first room built on the second floor. Since nothing else is finished on the second floor, I have in fact a large terrace looking out over the many houses of the neighborhood. My room consists of four brick walls—painted pink ("the only color I had") by our neighbor Octavio—and a roof made of sheets of metal. There is a door and a window, but the wind and the dust have free access to my home since the builders left a lot of open spaces where walls, window, door, and roof meet. With virtually no rain here and with little cold weather, my small place seems quite comfortable and pleasant.

I often have thought about having a *poustinia* or small building for prayer on the marketplace, and this new place seems to be just that. It is like a monk's cell between a large sea of houses and people.

. . . . From talking with Pablo, I learned that the two most treasured items in the house are the television and the refrigerator. When I came home from Mass with the three children, Pablo was standing on the street corner talking with a neighbor. When he saw me, he said: "Father, we are talking about the robberies on our street. At night, robbers drive their cars up, climb on the roof, and enter the house from above. They are after our televisions and refrigerators. The few things we have, they try to take away from us! It is becoming an unsafe place here."

A noticeable fear could be heard in Pablo's voice. A little later Sophia joined in the conversation, saying: "Can you believe it? They steal from the poor, those *rateros*."

¡Gracias!

If anything has affected me deeply since I have been living in Pamplona Alta, it has been the children . . . here I am surrounded by boys and girls running up to me, giving me kisses, climbing up to my shoulders, throwing balls at me, and constantly asking for some sign of interest in their lives.

The children always challenge me to live in the present. They want me to be with them here and now, and they find it hard to understand that I might have other things to do or think about. After all my experiences with psychotherapy, I suddenly have discovered the great healing power of children. Every time Pablito, Johnny, and Maria run up to welcome me, pick up my suitcase and bring it to my "roof-room," I marvel at their ability to be fully present to me. Their uninhibited expression of affection and their willingness to receive it pull me directly into the moment and invite me to celebrate life where it is found. . . . I now realize that only when I can enter with the children into their joy will I be able to enter also with them into their poverty and pain. God obviously wants me to walk into the world of suffering with a little child on each hand.

¡GRACIAS!

COCAINE AND ROSES

During the last few years, I have received several letters from Marist Sister Teresa asking for money to help some Peruvian ex-prisoners. Today Sister Teresa took me to Lurigancho, the huge prison where she works. It is hard to describe what I saw, heard and smelled. . . .

Lurigancho is a world within a world. About four thousand men live inside a small area surrounded by huge walls and watchtowers. They are there for reasons varying from murder to buying cocaine on the street. The majority of these men have never been sentenced and have no idea when their case will come to court or how long they will have to stay behind those walls. Some have been there for a few months, others for more than seven years; some are there for the first time, others old regulars for whom Lurigancho has become a second home. Some seem friendly and gentle, others silent and menacing.

Lurigancho impressed me as a microcosm of the extremes in life. Within the prison I visited several small libraries with helpful librarians. Everywhere were men weaving baskets, playing ball, sleeping in the sun, and standing on corners talking together. Less visible but no less real are the knives, guns, and drugs hidden in the corners, closets and cells. . . . Gangs fight each other, prisoners kill each other, groups pray together, men study together. There are meek, quiet, and unassuming people; there are also aggressive and dangerous men who are feared, avoided, or kept under control.

What struck me first was the enormous chaos. Once we had made our way through the gates, it seemed that all discipline was gone. Since most of the thirteen huge cellblocks were open, we could walk freely in, out and through. Prisoners were walking around with very little restriction and behaved as if they were in charge. Most of them were naked from the waist up; many just wore swimming trunks. Some showed big scars on their bodies, the result of self-inflicted cuts that had put them in hospital and allowed them to escape from torture. . . .

Often cellblocks fight with each other. Walls get broken down, windows smashed, and when there is enough alcohol around, people get wounded or killed. Once in a while things get so far out of hand that the *guardia republicana*, the police force, moves in. On February 2 the police carried out a wild and indiscriminately brutal assault on one cellblock. Tear gas was used and random shooting took place. During the four-hour rampage prisoners were severely beaten, tortured, and wounded. When it was all over, three men were dead.

While talking about this, one of the prisoners brought me to a little flower garden he had carefully cultivated. Proudly he showed me the lovely roses that had just come out. It was hard for me to put it all together. But that is Lurigancho. . . .

When we were let out through the heavy gates and stepped onto the bus to go home, I knew that only a very simple, pure, and holy person would be able to work with these men for any length of time. Just being there for four hours had made me see that Teresa must be such a person. She moved in this world without fear, open, practical, unsentimental, and with a deep sense of God's love. She saw it all clearly, but was not entangled in it. The men knew that she was one of the few who had no second motives. She was just there to be of help and that was all. Surrounded by the complexity of the dark world, the simple love of God can easily be discerned.

¡GRACIAS!

A LONG FIESTA WITH GOD

Gratitude is one of the most visible characteristics of the poor I have come to know. I am always surrounded by words of thanks: "thanks for your visit, your blessing, your sermon, your prayer, your gifts, your presence with us." Even the smallest and most necessary goods are a reason for gratitude.

This all-pervading gratitude is the basis for celebration. Not only are the poor grateful for life, but they also celebrate life constantly. A visit, a reunion, a simple meeting are always like little celebrations. Every time a new gift is recognized, there are songs or toasts, words of congratulation, or something to eat and drink. And every gift is shared. "Have a drink, take some fruit, eat our bread" is the response to every visit I make, and this is what I see people do for each other. All of life is a gift, a gift to be celebrated, a gift to be shared.

Thus the poor are a eucharistic people, people who know [how] to say thanks to God, to life, to each other. They may not come to Mass, they may not participate in many church celebrations. But in their hearts they are deeply religious because, for them, all of life is a long fiesta with God.

¡Gracias!

THE INCAS AND THE SUN GOD

This is my last day in Cuzco. John, Kathy, and I made a trip to the splendid Inca ruins in the area and to some churches and a museum in the town. More than ever before, I was impressed by the majestic beauty of the buildings of the Inca Empire. The gigantic temples, the watchposts, and ritual baths were the work of a people guided by the rule. "Do not lie, do not steal, and do not be lazy," and inspired by a powerful devotion to the Sun God and many other divinities. But, more than before, I was stunned by the total insensitivity of the Spanish conquerors to the culture and religion they found there.

It suddenly hit me how radical Gustavo Gutiérrez's liberation theology really is, because it is a theology that starts with the people and wants to recognize the deep spirituality of the Indians who live in this land. How different from what we saw today on our trip. There we witnessed a centuries-long disregard for any Indian religiosity, and a violent destruction of all that could possibly be a reminder of the Inca Gods. What an incredible pretension, what a cruelty, what a sacrilegious sin committed by people who claimed to come in the name of a God of forgiveness, love, and peace.

I wished I had the time to spend a whole day just sitting on the ruins of Sacsahuamán. These temple ruins overlooking the city of Cuzco, with its many churches built from its stones, make me ask the God of the sun, the moon, the stars, the rainbow, the lightening, the land, and the water to forgive what

Christians did in his name. Maybe the new spirituality of liberation is a creative form of repentance for the sins of our fathers. And I should not forget that these sins are closer to my own heart than I often want to confess. Some form of spiritual colonialism remains a constant temptation.

¡GRACIAS!

EPILOGUE

One way to express the spiritual crisis of our time is to say that most of us have an address but cannot be found there. We know where we belong, but we keep being pulled away in many directions, as if we were still homeless. "All these other things" keep demanding our attention. They lead us so far from home that we eventually forget our true address, that is, the place where we can be addressed.

Jesus responds to this condition of being filled yet unfulfilled, very busy yet unconnected, all over the place yet never at home. He wants to bring us to the place where we belong. But his call to live a spiritual life can only be heard when we are willing honestly to confess our own homeless and worrying existence and recognize its fragmenting effect on our daily life. Only then can a desire for our true home develop. It is of this desire that Jesus speaks when he says, "Do not worry. . . . Set your hearts on his kingdom first . . . and all these other things will be given you as well."

MAKING ALL THINGS NEW

I am a traveler on the way to a sacred place where God holds me in the palm of his hand.

(HENRI J. M. NOUWEN, 1932–1996)

Henri J.M. Nouwen, one of the most popular spiritual writers of our time, taught at Yale University, Harvard University, and the University of Notre Dame. From 1986 until his death in 1996, he taught and ministered to physically and mentally challenged men and women as a member of the L'Arche Daybreak community in Toronto, Canada. Learn more about Nouwen's life and works at www.henrinouwen.org.

Michael Ford, Ph.D., is the editor of *The Dance of Life* and *Eternal Seasons* (Ave Maria Press) and the author of several books including the award-winning *Wounded Prophet: A Portrait of Henri J. M. Nouwen.* He lives in England.